50 Brazilian Barbecue Recipes for Home

By: Kelly Johnson

Table of Contents

- Picanha (Sirloin Cap) Skewers:
    - Marinated picanha chunks grilled on skewers.
- Churrasco Chicken Hearts:
    - Seasoned and grilled chicken hearts, a popular Brazilian barbecue delicacy.
- Brazilian Grilled Shrimp:
    - Shrimp marinated in garlic, lime, and cilantro, then grilled.
- Garlic Buttered Ribeye:
    - Ribeye steaks brushed with garlic butter while grilling.
- Brazilian Pork Ribs:
    - Pork ribs seasoned with a Brazilian spice blend and slow-cooked on the grill.
- Grilled Sausage Skewers:
    - Assorted sausages grilled on skewers.
- Chicken Piri Piri:
    - Spicy grilled chicken with a Piri Piri marinade.
- Lamb Churrasco:
    - Lamb chops seasoned and grilled Brazilian style.
- Brazilian Steak with Chimichurri:
    - Grilled steak served with a zesty chimichurri sauce.
- Garlic-Lime Grilled Fish:
    - White fish fillets marinated in garlic and lime, then grilled.
- Brazilian Chicken Thighs.
    - Chicken thighs marinated in a mix of spices and grilled to perfection.
- Cilantro Lime Grilled Corn:
    - Corn on the cob grilled with cilantro and lime butter.
- Brazilian Pineapple Cinnamon Skewers:
    - Pineapple chunks sprinkled with cinnamon and grilled.
- Brazilian Lamb Chops with Mint Sauce:
    - Grilled lamb chops served with a refreshing mint sauce.
- Garlic Parmesan Grilled Artichokes:
    - Artichokes marinated in garlic, Parmesan, and herbs, then grilled.
- Brazilian Chicken Wings:
    - Chicken wings marinated in a spicy Brazilian sauce and grilled.

- Grilled Brazilian Beef Skewers:
    - Skewers of marinated beef chunks, grilled to perfection.
- Brazilian Sausage Sandwich:
    - Grilled Brazilian sausages in a sandwich with toppings.
- Spicy Grilled Shrimp Skewers:
    - Shrimp skewers with a spicy Brazilian marinade.
- Churrasco Pork Belly:
    - Crispy pork belly seasoned and grilled Brazilian style.
- Brazilian Garlic Butter Bread:
    - Bread brushed with garlic butter and grilled.
- Brazilian Skirt Steak:
    - Skirt steak marinated and grilled for a rich flavor.
- Grilled Eggplant with Chimichurri:
    - Eggplant slices grilled and served with chimichurri sauce.
- Brazilian Smoked Sausage:
    - Smoked sausages grilled to perfection.
- Brazilian Grilled Portobello Mushrooms:
    - Portobello mushrooms marinated and grilled.
- Brazilian Garlic-Lime Chicken Drumsticks:
    - Chicken drumsticks marinated in garlic, lime, and spices, then grilled.
- Cachaça-Glazed Grilled Pineapple:
    - Pineapple slices glazed with cachaça (Brazilian spirit) and grilled.
- Brazilian Garlic-Lime Butter Steak:
    - Steak topped with a garlic-lime butter sauce.
- Churrasco Picanha Burger:
    - Ground picanha formed into a flavorful burger, grilled to perfection.
- Brazilian Lemon-Garlic Swordfish:
    - Swordfish steaks marinated in lemon and garlic, then grilled.
- Brazilian BBQ Chicken Skewers:
    - Chicken skewers marinated in a barbecue-style sauce.
- Grilled Beef Heart:
    - Beef heart skewers marinated and grilled for a unique taste.
- Brazilian Grilled Cheese with Guava Paste:
    - Grilled cheese served with guava paste for a sweet and savory treat.
- Crispy Brazilian Pork Belly Skewers:
    - Pork belly skewers grilled to crispy perfection.
- Brazilian Grilled Zucchini:

- - Zucchini slices marinated and grilled until tender.
- Churrasco Lamb Leg:
  - Marinated and grilled lamb leg, a show-stopping dish.
- Brazilian Herb-Marinated Tofu Skewers:
  - Tofu cubes marinated in Brazilian herbs and grilled.
- Grilled Brazilian Halloumi:
  - Halloumi cheese slices grilled until golden.
- Brazilian Style Grilled Lobster Tails:
  - Lobster tails brushed with Brazilian-style seasoning and grilled.
- Churrasco-Style Grilled Okra:
  - Okra marinated and grilled for a tasty side dish.
- Brazilian BBQ Pulled Pork Sandwich:
  - Pulled pork with Brazilian barbecue sauce in a sandwich.
- Grilled Picanha Sandwich:
  - Sliced picanha steak served in a sandwich.
- Brazilian Spiced Grilled Cauliflower:
  - Cauliflower florets seasoned and grilled.
- Churrasco Beef Kebabs:
  - Beef kebabs with a churrasco-style marinade.
- Brazilian Guava Glazed Chicken Wings:
  - Chicken wings glazed with a sweet and spicy guava sauce.
- Grilled Brazilian Sardines:
  - Fresh sardines marinated and grilled.
- Brazilian Pork Tenderloin with Mango Salsa:
  - Pork tenderloin grilled and topped with a refreshing mango salsa.
- Churrasco-Style Grilled Potatoes:
  - Potatoes seasoned and grilled Brazilian style.
- Brazilian Cinnamon Sugar Grilled Bananas:
  - Bananas grilled with cinnamon sugar for a sweet dessert.
- Churrasco-Style Grilled Mushrooms:
  - Assorted mushrooms marinated and grilled for a flavorful side.

Picanha (Sirloin Cap) Skewers

Ingredients:

For the Picanha Marinade:

- 2 pounds picanha (sirloin cap), cut into 1-inch cubes
- 4 cloves garlic, minced
- 1/4 cup olive oil
- 2 tablespoons red wine vinegar
- 2 tablespoons soy sauce
- 1 tablespoon Dijon mustard
- 1 teaspoon smoked paprika
- Salt and black pepper to taste

For Skewers:

- Wooden or metal skewers, soaked if wooden

Instructions:

Prepare the Picanha Marinade:
- In a bowl, whisk together minced garlic, olive oil, red wine vinegar, soy sauce, Dijon mustard, smoked paprika, salt, and black pepper.

Marinate the Picanha:
- Place the picanha cubes in a large resealable plastic bag or a shallow dish. Pour the marinade over the meat, ensuring each piece is well coated. Seal the bag or cover the dish and refrigerate for at least 2 hours or overnight for optimal flavor.

Preheat the Grill:
- Preheat your grill to medium-high heat.

Skewer the Picanha:
- Thread the marinated picanha cubes onto skewers, ensuring an even distribution.

Grill the Skewers:

- Place the skewers on the preheated grill. Grill for about 8-10 minutes, turning occasionally, or until the picanha is cooked to your desired level of doneness.

Baste with Marinade (Optional):
- Optionally, you can baste the skewers with the remaining marinade during the last few minutes of grilling for extra flavor.

Rest and Serve:
- Remove the skewers from the grill and let them rest for a few minutes before serving.

Garnish (Optional):
- Garnish with chopped fresh parsley or cilantro, if desired.

Serve:
- Serve the Picanha Skewers hot, either as an appetizer or as a main course with your favorite side dishes.

Enjoy:
- Enjoy these succulent Picanha Skewers, a Brazilian barbecue classic, bursting with rich flavors from the marinade and the grilling process.

Note: Picanha is known for its unique fat cap. Ensure that each skewer includes a good balance of meat and fat for the authentic taste and texture of Brazilian barbecue.

Churrasco Chicken Hearts

Ingredients:

- 1 pound chicken hearts, cleaned and trimmed
- 3 tablespoons olive oil
- 4 cloves garlic, minced
- 2 tablespoons fresh parsley, finely chopped
- 1 tablespoon red wine vinegar
- 1 teaspoon smoked paprika
- 1 teaspoon ground cumin
- Salt and black pepper to taste
- Wooden or metal skewers, soaked if wooden

Instructions:

Prepare the Marinade:
- In a bowl, whisk together olive oil, minced garlic, chopped parsley, red wine vinegar, smoked paprika, ground cumin, salt, and black pepper to create the marinade.

Clean and Trim Chicken Hearts:
- Ensure the chicken hearts are cleaned and trimmed. Remove any excess fat or connective tissue.

Marinate the Chicken Hearts:
- Place the cleaned chicken hearts in a large bowl or a resealable plastic bag. Pour the marinade over the chicken hearts, making sure each heart is well coated. Marinate in the refrigerator for at least 1 hour, allowing the flavors to infuse.

Preheat the Grill:
- Preheat your grill to medium-high heat.

Skewer the Chicken Hearts:
- Thread the marinated chicken hearts onto skewers, distributing them evenly.

Grill the Skewers:
- Place the skewers on the preheated grill. Grill for about 4-6 minutes per side, turning occasionally, until the chicken hearts are cooked through and have a nice char.

Baste with Marinade (Optional):

- Optionally, you can baste the chicken hearts with the remaining marinade during the last few minutes of grilling for extra flavor.

Check for Doneness:
- Ensure the chicken hearts are fully cooked, with no pinkness in the center.

Rest and Serve:
- Remove the skewers from the grill and let them rest for a few minutes.

Garnish (Optional):
- Garnish with additional chopped parsley if desired.

Serve:
- Serve the Churrasco Chicken Hearts hot as a flavorful and unique appetizer or part of a Brazilian barbecue feast.

Enjoy:
- Enjoy the rich and savory taste of Churrasco Chicken Hearts, a delicacy in Brazilian barbecue culture.

Brazilian Grilled Shrimp

Ingredients:

- 1 pound large shrimp, peeled and deveined
- 3 tablespoons olive oil
- 3 cloves garlic, minced
- 2 tablespoons fresh cilantro, chopped
- 1 tablespoon lime juice
- 1 teaspoon smoked paprika
- 1 teaspoon ground cumin
- 1/2 teaspoon red pepper flakes (adjust to taste)
- Salt and black pepper to taste
- Wooden or metal skewers, soaked if wooden
- Lime wedges for serving

Instructions:

Prepare the Marinade:
- In a bowl, mix together olive oil, minced garlic, chopped cilantro, lime juice, smoked paprika, ground cumin, red pepper flakes, salt, and black pepper to create the marinade.

Marinate the Shrimp:
- Place the peeled and deveined shrimp in a large bowl. Pour the marinade over the shrimp, ensuring each piece is well coated. Marinate in the refrigerator for 30 minutes to 1 hour.

Preheat the Grill:
- Preheat your grill to medium-high heat.

Skewer the Shrimp:
- Thread the marinated shrimp onto skewers, evenly distributing them.

Grill the Skewers:
- Place the skewers on the preheated grill. Grill for approximately 2-3 minutes per side or until the shrimp turn pink and opaque with a slight char.

Baste with Marinade (Optional):
- Optionally, you can baste the shrimp with the remaining marinade during the last few minutes of grilling for extra flavor.

Check for Doneness:

- Ensure the shrimp are fully cooked but be cautious not to overcook to maintain their tenderness.

Remove from Grill:
- Remove the skewers from the grill and place them on a serving platter.

Garnish (Optional):
- Garnish with additional chopped cilantro and serve with lime wedges.

Serve:
- Serve the Brazilian Grilled Shrimp hot as a delightful appetizer or as part of a Brazilian barbecue spread.

Enjoy:
- Enjoy the vibrant flavors of these grilled shrimp with a touch of Brazilian flair. Perfect for sharing with friends and family.

Garlic Buttered Ribeye

Ingredients:

- 2 ribeye steaks (about 1.5 inches thick)
- Salt and black pepper to taste
- 2 tablespoons olive oil
- 4 tablespoons unsalted butter
- 4 cloves garlic, minced
- 2 sprigs fresh rosemary (optional)
- Fresh parsley, chopped, for garnish (optional)

Instructions:

Bring Ribeye to Room Temperature:
- Take the ribeye steaks out of the refrigerator at least 30 minutes before cooking to bring them to room temperature.

Preheat the Grill or Pan:
- Preheat your grill or a cast-iron pan over medium-high heat.

Season the Ribeye:
- Pat the ribeye steaks dry with paper towels. Season both sides generously with salt and black pepper.

Brush with Olive Oil:
- Brush each side of the steaks with olive oil to promote a nice sear.

Grill or Pan-Sear the Ribeye:
- Place the ribeye steaks on the preheated grill or pan. Grill for about 4-5 minutes per side for medium-rare, adjusting the time based on your desired doneness.

Add Butter and Garlic:
- In the last 2 minutes of cooking, add 2 tablespoons of butter to the pan or grill. Add minced garlic and fresh rosemary if using. Allow the butter to melt and infuse with the garlic.

Baste the Ribeye:
- Using a spoon, continuously baste the ribeye with the garlic-infused butter. Ensure the garlic doesn't burn but becomes aromatic.

Check for Doneness:
- Use a meat thermometer to check the internal temperature. For medium-rare, aim for about 135°F (57°C).

Rest the Ribeye:
- Remove the ribeye steaks from the grill or pan and let them rest on a cutting board for at least 5 minutes. This allows the juices to redistribute.

Slice and Serve:
- Slice the ribeye against the grain into 1/2-inch thick slices.

Garnish and Enjoy:
- Garnish with chopped fresh parsley if desired. Serve the Garlic Buttered Ribeye slices hot.

Optional: Make Extra Garlic Butter for Dipping:
- If you like, you can make an extra batch of garlic butter for dipping.

Enjoy:
- Indulge in the rich and flavorful Garlic Buttered Ribeye, a classic and mouthwatering steak preparation.

Brazilian Pork Ribs

Ingredients:

For the Marinade:

- 2 racks of baby back pork ribs
- 1/4 cup olive oil
- 1/4 cup soy sauce
- 1/4 cup orange juice
- 3 tablespoons honey
- 4 cloves garlic, minced
- 1 tablespoon ground cumin
- 1 tablespoon smoked paprika
- 1 teaspoon dried oregano
- Salt and black pepper to taste

For the Glaze:

- 1/2 cup barbecue sauce (Brazilian-style if available)
- 2 tablespoons honey
- 1 tablespoon Dijon mustard
- 1 tablespoon apple cider vinegar

Optional:

- Lime wedges for serving
- Chopped fresh cilantro for garnish

Instructions:

Prepare the Ribs:
- Remove the membrane from the back of the ribs for better flavor penetration. Place the ribs in a large baking dish.

Make the Marinade:
- In a bowl, whisk together olive oil, soy sauce, orange juice, honey, minced garlic, ground cumin, smoked paprika, dried oregano, salt, and black pepper to create the marinade.

Marinate the Ribs:

- Pour the marinade over the ribs, ensuring they are well coated. Cover the dish and refrigerate for at least 4 hours or overnight.

Preheat the Grill:
- Preheat your grill to medium-high heat.

Grill the Ribs:
- Remove the ribs from the marinade and let excess marinade drip off. Place the ribs on the preheated grill and cook for about 30-40 minutes, turning occasionally, until the ribs are cooked through and have a nice char.

Make the Glaze:
- In a small saucepan, combine barbecue sauce, honey, Dijon mustard, and apple cider vinegar. Heat over medium heat until the glaze is well combined and slightly thickened.

Glaze the Ribs:
- Brush the ribs with the glaze during the last 10-15 minutes of grilling, allowing the glaze to caramelize on the ribs.

Check for Doneness:
- Ensure the ribs are fully cooked, and the internal temperature reaches at least 145°F (63°C).

Rest and Slice:
- Remove the ribs from the grill and let them rest for a few minutes before slicing.

Garnish and Serve:
- Garnish with chopped fresh cilantro if desired. Serve the Brazilian Pork Ribs hot with lime wedges on the side.

Enjoy:
- Enjoy the succulent and flavorful Brazilian Pork Ribs, a perfect addition to your barbecue feast.

Grilled Sausage Skewers

Ingredients:

- 1 pound your favorite sausages (chorizo, Italian, bratwurst, etc.), sliced into bite-sized pieces
- 1 red bell pepper, cut into chunks
- 1 yellow bell pepper, cut into chunks
- 1 red onion, cut into chunks
- 2 tablespoons olive oil
- 2 teaspoons smoked paprika
- 1 teaspoon dried oregano
- Salt and black pepper to taste
- Wooden or metal skewers, soaked if wooden

Instructions:

Preheat the Grill:
- Preheat your grill to medium-high heat.

Prepare the Sausages and Vegetables:
- Slice the sausages into bite-sized pieces and cut the bell peppers and red onion into chunks.

Make the Marinade:
- In a bowl, mix together olive oil, smoked paprika, dried oregano, salt, and black pepper to create the marinade.

Marinate the Sausages and Vegetables:
- Place the sausage pieces, bell pepper chunks, and red onion chunks in a large bowl. Pour the marinade over them and toss to coat evenly. Let it marinate for at least 15-30 minutes.

Assemble the Skewers:
- Thread the marinated sausage pieces, bell pepper chunks, and red onion chunks onto the skewers, alternating for a colorful presentation.

Grill the Skewers:
- Place the skewers on the preheated grill. Grill for about 10-15 minutes, turning occasionally, until the sausages are cooked through, and the vegetables have a nice char.

Check for Doneness:

- Ensure the sausages are cooked through, and the internal temperature reaches a safe level according to the type of sausage used.

Remove from Grill:
- Once cooked, remove the skewers from the grill and let them rest for a couple of minutes.

Serve:
- Serve the Grilled Sausage Skewers hot as a delicious and easy-to-eat appetizer or main dish.

Optional: Dipping Sauce:
- Prepare a simple dipping sauce with a mixture of barbecue sauce, mustard, and honey for extra flavor.

Enjoy:
- Enjoy these tasty Grilled Sausage Skewers as a crowd-pleasing dish for your barbecue or outdoor gathering.

Chicken Piri Piri

Ingredients:

For the Piri Piri Marinade:

- 4 bone-in, skin-on chicken thighs
- 4 cloves garlic, minced
- 2 tablespoons fresh lemon juice
- 2 tablespoons olive oil
- 2 teaspoons paprika
- 1 teaspoon dried oregano
- 1 teaspoon red pepper flakes (adjust to taste)
- 1 teaspoon ground cumin
- Salt and black pepper to taste

For the Piri Piri Sauce:

- 2 tablespoons olive oil
- 2 tablespoons hot sauce (adjust to taste)
- 1 tablespoon red wine vinegar
- 1 tablespoon honey or maple syrup
- Salt to taste

Instructions:

Prepare the Chicken:
- Pat the chicken thighs dry with paper towels. Make a few shallow slashes on the skin side of each thigh to allow the marinade to penetrate.

Make the Piri Piri Marinade:
- In a bowl, mix together minced garlic, fresh lemon juice, olive oil, paprika, dried oregano, red pepper flakes, ground cumin, salt, and black pepper to create the marinade.

Marinate the Chicken:
- Rub the chicken thighs with the Piri Piri marinade, ensuring the marinade gets into the slashes. Marinate for at least 1 hour, or preferably overnight in the refrigerator.

Preheat the Grill:
- Preheat your grill to medium-high heat.

Grill the Chicken:
- Remove the chicken thighs from the marinade and place them on the preheated grill. Grill for about 25-30 minutes, turning occasionally, until the chicken is cooked through, and the skin is crispy.

Make the Piri Piri Sauce:
- While the chicken is grilling, prepare the Piri Piri sauce. In a small saucepan, combine olive oil, hot sauce, red wine vinegar, honey or maple syrup, and salt. Heat over low heat until well combined.

Baste with Piri Piri Sauce:
- During the last 10 minutes of grilling, baste the chicken thighs with the Piri Piri sauce, ensuring they are coated on all sides.

Check for Doneness:
- Ensure the chicken thighs are fully cooked, with no pinkness near the bone, and the internal temperature reaches at least 165°F (74°C).

Remove from Grill:
- Once cooked, remove the chicken thighs from the grill and let them rest for a few minutes.

Serve:
- Serve the Chicken Piri Piri hot, drizzled with additional Piri Piri sauce if desired.

Garnish (Optional):
- Garnish with fresh chopped cilantro or parsley for a burst of freshness.

Enjoy:
- Enjoy the bold and spicy flavors of Chicken Piri Piri, a classic Portuguese-inspired dish that's perfect for a barbecue or grilled dinner.

Lamb Churrasco

Ingredients:

For the Lamb Marinade:

- 2 pounds lamb chops or lamb skewers
- 1/4 cup olive oil
- 4 cloves garlic, minced
- 2 tablespoons red wine vinegar
- 1 tablespoon dried oregano
- 1 teaspoon smoked paprika
- 1 teaspoon ground cumin
- Salt and black pepper to taste

For the Chimichurri Sauce:

- 1 cup fresh parsley, finely chopped
- 1/4 cup fresh cilantro, finely chopped
- 3 cloves garlic, minced
- 1/2 cup extra-virgin olive oil
- 2 tablespoons red wine vinegar
- 1 teaspoon dried oregano
- 1/2 teaspoon red pepper flakes (adjust to taste)
- Salt and black pepper to taste

Instructions:

Prepare the Lamb:
- If using lamb chops, ensure they are well-trimmed. If using skewers, thread the lamb pieces onto the skewers.

Make the Lamb Marinade:
- In a bowl, whisk together olive oil, minced garlic, red wine vinegar, dried oregano, smoked paprika, ground cumin, salt, and black pepper to create the marinade.

Marinate the Lamb:

- Place the lamb chops or skewers in a shallow dish. Pour the marinade over them, ensuring each piece is well coated. Marinate for at least 1-2 hours, or overnight in the refrigerator for enhanced flavor.

Preheat the Grill:
- Preheat your grill to medium-high heat.

Grill the Lamb:
- Remove the lamb from the marinade and let excess marinade drip off. Place the lamb on the preheated grill. Grill for about 8-10 minutes for lamb chops or 10-15 minutes for skewers, turning occasionally, until the lamb is cooked to your desired level of doneness.

Make the Chimichurri Sauce:
- While the lamb is grilling, prepare the chimichurri sauce. In a bowl, mix together finely chopped parsley, finely chopped cilantro, minced garlic, extra-virgin olive oil, red wine vinegar, dried oregano, red pepper flakes, salt, and black pepper.

Serve:
- Once the lamb is cooked, remove it from the grill and let it rest for a few minutes.

Garnish and Drizzle:
- Garnish the lamb with a sprinkle of fresh parsley and cilantro. Drizzle the chimichurri sauce generously over the lamb.

Serve Hot:
- Serve the Lamb Churrasco hot, with additional chimichurri sauce on the side for dipping.

Enjoy:
- Enjoy the rich and savory flavors of Lamb Churrasco with the vibrant and herbaceous chimichurri sauce, a delightful dish perfect for a barbecue or special occasion.

Brazilian Steak with Chimichurri

Ingredients:

For the Steak:

- 2 pounds beef sirloin or ribeye steaks
- Salt and black pepper to taste

For the Marinade:

- 1/4 cup olive oil
- 4 cloves garlic, minced
- 2 tablespoons soy sauce
- 2 tablespoons red wine vinegar
- 1 tablespoon smoked paprika
- 1 tablespoon dried oregano
- 1 teaspoon ground cumin

For the Chimichurri Sauce:

- 1 cup fresh parsley, finely chopped
- 1/4 cup fresh cilantro, finely chopped
- 3 cloves garlic, minced
- 1/2 cup extra-virgin olive oil
- 2 tablespoons red wine vinegar
- 1 teaspoon dried oregano
- 1/2 teaspoon red pepper flakes (adjust to taste)
- Salt and black pepper to taste

Instructions:

Prepare the Steak:
- Pat the steaks dry with paper towels. Season both sides with salt and black pepper.

Make the Marinade:

- In a bowl, whisk together olive oil, minced garlic, soy sauce, red wine vinegar, smoked paprika, dried oregano, and ground cumin.

Marinate the Steak:
- Place the steaks in a shallow dish and pour the marinade over them. Ensure each steak is well coated. Marinate for at least 1-2 hours, or overnight in the refrigerator for deeper flavor.

Preheat the Grill:
- Preheat your grill to medium-high heat.

Grill the Steak:
- Remove the steaks from the marinade, letting excess marinade drip off. Place the steaks on the preheated grill. Grill for about 4-6 minutes per side for medium-rare, adjusting the time based on your desired doneness.

Make the Chimichurri Sauce:
- While the steak is grilling, prepare the chimichurri sauce. In a bowl, mix together finely chopped parsley, finely chopped cilantro, minced garlic, extra-virgin olive oil, red wine vinegar, dried oregano, red pepper flakes, salt, and black pepper.

Rest the Steak:
- Once the steak is cooked, remove it from the grill and let it rest for a few minutes.

Slice and Serve:
- Slice the steak against the grain into 1/2-inch thick slices.

Drizzle with Chimichurri:
- Drizzle the chimichurri sauce generously over the sliced steak.

Garnish and Serve:
- Garnish with additional chopped parsley or cilantro if desired. Serve the Brazilian Steak with Chimichurri hot.

Enjoy:
- Enjoy the robust flavors of Brazilian Steak with the herby and tangy goodness of chimichurri, a delightful dish that captures the essence of Brazilian barbecue.

Garlic-Lime Grilled Fish

Ingredients:

- 4 fish fillets (such as tilapia, cod, or snapper)
- Salt and black pepper to taste
- 3 cloves garlic, minced
- Zest of 1 lime
- Juice of 2 limes
- 2 tablespoons olive oil
- 1 teaspoon ground cumin
- 1 teaspoon paprika
- 1/2 teaspoon cayenne pepper (adjust to taste)
- Fresh cilantro, chopped, for garnish
- Lime wedges for serving

Instructions:

Prepare the Fish:
- Pat the fish fillets dry with paper towels. Season both sides with salt and black pepper.

Make the Marinade:
- In a bowl, combine minced garlic, lime zest, lime juice, olive oil, ground cumin, paprika, and cayenne pepper to create the marinade.

Marinate the Fish:
- Place the fish fillets in a shallow dish. Pour the marinade over them, ensuring each fillet is well coated. Marinate for at least 30 minutes to allow the flavors to infuse.

Preheat the Grill:
- Preheat your grill to medium-high heat.

Grill the Fish:
- Remove the fish from the marinade, letting excess marinade drip off. Place the fillets on the preheated grill. Grill for about 3-4 minutes per side, or until the fish is cooked through and easily flakes with a fork.

Check for Doneness:
- Ensure the fish is fully cooked but still moist. The internal temperature should reach 145°F (63°C).

Garnish:

- Garnish the grilled fish with chopped fresh cilantro.

Serve:
- Serve the Garlic-Lime Grilled Fish hot, with lime wedges on the side for squeezing.

Optional: Extra Marinade Drizzle:
- If desired, drizzle some of the reserved marinade over the grilled fish before serving.

Enjoy:
- Enjoy the light and zesty flavors of Garlic-Lime Grilled Fish, a simple and delicious dish that's perfect for a quick and healthy meal.

Brazilian Chicken Thighs

Ingredients:

For the Chicken Marinade:

- 8 bone-in, skin-on chicken thighs
- 4 cloves garlic, minced
- 2 tablespoons olive oil
- 2 tablespoons lime juice
- 1 tablespoon paprika
- 1 tablespoon ground cumin
- 1 teaspoon dried oregano
- Salt and black pepper to taste

For the Chimichurri Sauce:

- 1 cup fresh parsley, finely chopped
- 1/4 cup fresh cilantro, finely chopped
- 3 cloves garlic, minced
- 1/2 cup extra-virgin olive oil
- 2 tablespoons red wine vinegar
- 1 teaspoon dried oregano
- 1/2 teaspoon red pepper flakes (adjust to taste)
- Salt and black pepper to taste

Instructions:

Prepare the Chicken:
- Pat the chicken thighs dry with paper towels. Place them in a large bowl or a shallow dish.

Make the Chicken Marinade:
- In a bowl, mix together minced garlic, olive oil, lime juice, paprika, ground cumin, dried oregano, salt, and black pepper to create the marinade.

Marinate the Chicken:
- Pour the marinade over the chicken thighs, ensuring each thigh is well coated. Marinate for at least 30 minutes to allow the flavors to infuse.

Preheat the Grill:
- Preheat your grill to medium-high heat.

Grill the Chicken:
- Remove the chicken thighs from the marinade, letting excess marinade drip off. Place the thighs on the preheated grill. Grill for about 15-20 minutes, turning occasionally, until the chicken is cooked through and has a nice char on the skin.

Check for Doneness:
- Ensure the chicken thighs are fully cooked, with no pinkness near the bone, and the internal temperature reaches at least 165°F (74°C).

Make the Chimichurri Sauce:
- While the chicken is grilling, prepare the chimichurri sauce. In a bowl, mix together finely chopped parsley, finely chopped cilantro, minced garlic, extra-virgin olive oil, red wine vinegar, dried oregano, red pepper flakes, salt, and black pepper.

Serve:
- Once the chicken thighs are cooked, remove them from the grill.

Garnish with Chimichurri:
- Drizzle the chimichurri sauce generously over the grilled chicken thighs.

Garnish and Serve:
- Garnish with additional chopped fresh parsley or cilantro if desired. Serve the Brazilian Chicken Thighs hot.

Enjoy:
- Enjoy the vibrant and flavorful Brazilian Chicken Thighs with the zesty kick of chimichurri sauce, a delicious dish that captures the essence of Brazilian cuisine.

Cilantro Lime Grilled Corn

Ingredients:

- 4 ears of corn, husked
- 2 tablespoons unsalted butter, melted
- 2 tablespoons fresh cilantro, finely chopped
- Zest of 1 lime
- Juice of 1 lime
- Salt and black pepper to taste
- Grated Parmesan cheese (optional, for serving)

Instructions:

Preheat the Grill:
- Preheat your grill to medium-high heat.

Prepare the Corn:
- Husk the corn and remove any silk. Rinse the corn under cold water.

Grill the Corn:
- Place the corn on the preheated grill. Grill for about 10-15 minutes, turning occasionally, until the corn is cooked and has a slight char.

Make the Cilantro Lime Butter:
- In a small bowl, mix together melted butter, finely chopped cilantro, lime zest, and lime juice to create the cilantro lime butter.

Brush the Corn:
- During the last few minutes of grilling, brush the corn with the cilantro lime butter, ensuring each ear is well coated.

Season with Salt and Pepper:
- Sprinkle salt and black pepper over the grilled corn to taste.

Optional: Grated Parmesan Cheese:
- If desired, sprinkle grated Parmesan cheese over the corn for an extra savory kick.

Serve:
- Remove the corn from the grill and place it on a serving platter.

Garnish (Optional):
- Garnish with additional chopped cilantro and lime wedges if desired.

Enjoy:

- Serve the Cilantro Lime Grilled Corn hot as a flavorful and vibrant side dish, perfect for summer gatherings or barbecues.

Brazilian Pineapple Cinnamon Skewers

Ingredients:

- 1 large pineapple, peeled, cored, and cut into chunks
- 2 tablespoons honey
- 1 teaspoon ground cinnamon
- Wooden or metal skewers

Instructions:

Preheat the Grill:
- Preheat your grill to medium-high heat.

Prepare the Pineapple:
- Peel the pineapple, remove the core, and cut it into bite-sized chunks.

Make the Cinnamon Honey Glaze:
- In a small bowl, mix together honey and ground cinnamon to create the glaze.

Skewer the Pineapple:
- Thread the pineapple chunks onto the skewers, leaving some space between each piece.

Brush with Glaze:
- Brush the pineapple skewers with the cinnamon honey glaze, ensuring each piece is coated.

Grill the Pineapple:
- Place the skewers on the preheated grill. Grill for about 5-7 minutes, turning occasionally, until the pineapple has a nice caramelized char.

Brush with More Glaze:
- During the last few minutes of grilling, brush the pineapple skewers with additional cinnamon honey glaze for extra flavor.

Check for Caramelization:
- Ensure the pineapple has caramelized edges and is heated through.

Remove from Grill:
- Once grilled to your liking, remove the pineapple skewers from the grill.

Serve:
- Place the grilled pineapple skewers on a serving platter.

Garnish (Optional):
- Garnish with a sprinkle of ground cinnamon for a decorative touch.

Enjoy:

- Serve the Brazilian Pineapple Cinnamon Skewers hot as a delightful and naturally sweet dessert or snack. They can be enjoyed on their own or paired with a scoop of vanilla ice cream for an extra treat.

Brazilian Lamb Chops with Mint Sauce

Ingredients:

For the Lamb Chops:

- 8 lamb chops, frenched
- 3 cloves garlic, minced
- 2 tablespoons olive oil
- 1 tablespoon ground cumin
- 1 tablespoon smoked paprika
- Salt and black pepper to taste

For the Mint Sauce:

- 1 cup fresh mint leaves, chopped
- 1/4 cup fresh cilantro, chopped
- 3 tablespoons olive oil
- 2 tablespoons red wine vinegar
- 1 tablespoon honey
- Salt and black pepper to taste

Instructions:

Prepare the Lamb Chops:
- In a bowl, mix together minced garlic, olive oil, ground cumin, smoked paprika, salt, and black pepper to create the marinade.

Marinate the Lamb Chops:
- Place the lamb chops in a shallow dish and rub them with the marinade. Ensure each chop is well coated. Marinate for at least 30 minutes to allow the flavors to infuse.

Preheat the Grill:
- Preheat your grill to medium-high heat.

Grill the Lamb Chops:
- Remove the lamb chops from the marinade, letting excess marinade drip off. Place the chops on the preheated grill. Grill for about 4-6 minutes per side, or until the lamb is cooked to your desired level of doneness.

Make the Mint Sauce:

- While the lamb is grilling, prepare the mint sauce. In a bowl, mix together chopped mint leaves, chopped cilantro, olive oil, red wine vinegar, honey, salt, and black pepper.

Rest the Lamb Chops:
- Once the lamb chops are cooked, remove them from the grill and let them rest for a few minutes.

Serve with Mint Sauce:
- Drizzle the mint sauce over the grilled lamb chops before serving.

Garnish and Serve:
- Garnish with additional fresh mint leaves or cilantro if desired. Serve the Brazilian Lamb Chops with Mint Sauce hot.

Enjoy:
- Enjoy the succulent and flavorful Brazilian Lamb Chops with the refreshing mint sauce, a delicious dish that's perfect for a special occasion or barbecue.

Garlic Parmesan Grilled Artichokes

Ingredients:

- 4 large artichokes
- 2 lemons, halved
- 1/4 cup olive oil
- 4 cloves garlic, minced
- 1/2 cup grated Parmesan cheese
- Salt and black pepper to taste
- Fresh parsley, chopped (for garnish)

Instructions:

Prepare the Artichokes:
- Trim the stems and tough outer leaves of the artichokes. Cut the top inch off each artichoke and use kitchen scissors to trim the sharp tips from the remaining leaves.

Steam the Artichokes:
- Fill a large pot with about 2 inches of water. Place a steamer basket in the pot. Squeeze the juice from one lemon into the water and add the lemon halves to the pot. Bring the water to a simmer over medium heat. Place the artichokes in the steamer basket, cover, and steam for about 20-25 minutes or until the leaves can be easily pulled off.

Prepare the Garlic Parmesan Mixture:
- In a small bowl, mix together olive oil, minced garlic, grated Parmesan cheese, salt, and black pepper.

Preheat the Grill:
- Preheat your grill to medium-high heat.

Cut Artichokes in Half:
- Once the artichokes are steamed, cut them in half lengthwise. Use a spoon to scoop out the fuzzy choke from the center.

Brush with Garlic Parmesan Mixture:
- Brush the cut sides of the artichokes with the garlic Parmesan mixture.

Grill the Artichokes:
- Place the artichokes on the preheated grill, cut side down. Grill for about 5-7 minutes, or until they develop grill marks and are heated through.

Serve:

- Squeeze the juice from the remaining lemon over the grilled artichokes. Sprinkle with fresh chopped parsley for garnish.

Enjoy:
- Serve the Garlic Parmesan Grilled Artichokes as a flavorful and elegant appetizer or side dish. Enjoy the delicious combination of smoky grilled flavor and savory Parmesan goodness.

Brazilian Chicken Wings

Ingredients:

For the Marinade:

- 2 pounds chicken wings, split at joints, tips discarded
- 3 cloves garlic, minced
- 1 tablespoon olive oil
- 2 tablespoons lime juice
- 1 tablespoon paprika
- 1 tablespoon ground cumin
- 1 teaspoon dried oregano
- Salt and black pepper to taste

For the Sauce:

- 1/4 cup unsalted butter
- 1/4 cup hot sauce (adjust to taste)
- 2 tablespoons honey
- 1 tablespoon lime juice
- 1 teaspoon smoked paprika
- 1 teaspoon garlic powder
- Salt to taste

For Garnish (Optional):

- Fresh cilantro, chopped
- Lime wedges

Instructions:

Marinate the Chicken Wings:
- In a bowl, mix together minced garlic, olive oil, lime juice, paprika, ground cumin, dried oregano, salt, and black pepper to create the marinade. Coat the chicken wings with the marinade and let them marinate for at least 30 minutes, or preferably, refrigerate overnight for enhanced flavor.

Preheat the Grill:
- Preheat your grill to medium-high heat.

Grill the Chicken Wings:

- Remove the chicken wings from the marinade and let excess marinade drip off. Place the wings on the preheated grill. Grill for about 20-25 minutes, turning occasionally, until the wings are cooked through and have a nice char.

Make the Sauce:
- In a saucepan, melt the butter. Add hot sauce, honey, lime juice, smoked paprika, garlic powder, and salt. Stir well and simmer for a few minutes until the sauce thickens slightly.

Toss the Wings in Sauce:
- Once the chicken wings are cooked, toss them in the prepared sauce, ensuring they are well coated.

Garnish (Optional):
- Garnish the Brazilian Chicken Wings with chopped fresh cilantro and serve with lime wedges on the side.

Serve:
- Arrange the wings on a serving platter.

Enjoy:
- Enjoy the bold and spicy flavors of Brazilian Chicken Wings, perfect for a barbecue, game day, or any festive gathering.

Grilled Brazilian Beef Skewers

Ingredients:

For the Marinade:

- 2 pounds beef sirloin or flank steak, cut into 1-inch cubes
- 4 cloves garlic, minced
- 1/4 cup olive oil
- 2 tablespoons soy sauce
- 2 tablespoons lime juice
- 1 tablespoon smoked paprika
- 1 tablespoon ground cumin
- 1 teaspoon dried oregano
- Salt and black pepper to taste

For the Chimichurri Sauce:

- 1 cup fresh parsley, finely chopped
- 1/4 cup fresh cilantro, finely chopped
- 3 cloves garlic, minced
- 1/2 cup extra-virgin olive oil
- 2 tablespoons red wine vinegar
- 1 teaspoon dried oregano
- 1/2 teaspoon red pepper flakes (adjust to taste)
- Salt and black pepper to taste

Instructions:

Prepare the Beef:
- Cut the beef into 1-inch cubes, ensuring they are similar in size for even cooking.

Make the Marinade:
- In a bowl, whisk together minced garlic, olive oil, soy sauce, lime juice, smoked paprika, ground cumin, dried oregano, salt, and black pepper to create the marinade.

Marinate the Beef:

- Place the beef cubes in a shallow dish and pour the marinade over them. Ensure each piece is well coated. Marinate for at least 30 minutes, or refrigerate overnight for deeper flavor.

Preheat the Grill:
- Preheat your grill to medium-high heat.

Skewer the Beef:
- Thread the marinated beef cubes onto skewers, leaving a small space between each piece.

Grill the Skewers:
- Place the skewers on the preheated grill. Grill for about 8-10 minutes, turning occasionally, until the beef is cooked to your desired level of doneness.

Make the Chimichurri Sauce:
- While the beef is grilling, prepare the chimichurri sauce. In a bowl, mix together finely chopped parsley, finely chopped cilantro, minced garlic, extra-virgin olive oil, red wine vinegar, dried oregano, red pepper flakes, salt, and black pepper.

Serve with Chimichurri:
- Once the beef skewers are cooked, remove them from the grill. Serve the skewers with a generous drizzle of chimichurri sauce.

Garnish and Enjoy:
- Garnish with additional fresh herbs if desired. Enjoy the Grilled Brazilian Beef Skewers with the vibrant and flavorful chimichurri sauce.

Brazilian Sausage Sandwich

Ingredients:

For the Sausage:

- 1 pound Brazilian sausages (linguiça), sliced lengthwise
- Olive oil for brushing

For the Chimichurri Mayo:

- 1/2 cup mayonnaise
- 1/4 cup fresh parsley, finely chopped
- 2 tablespoons fresh cilantro, finely chopped
- 2 cloves garlic, minced
- 1 tablespoon red wine vinegar
- 1 teaspoon dried oregano
- Salt and black pepper to taste

For the Sandwich:

- 4 Portuguese rolls or crusty rolls
- 1 large onion, thinly sliced and caramelized
- 1 red bell pepper, thinly sliced and grilled

Instructions:

Preheat the Grill:
- Preheat your grill to medium-high heat.

Grill the Sausages:
- Brush the sliced Brazilian sausages with olive oil. Grill them on the preheated grill until they are cooked through and have a nice char, about 10-15 minutes.

Make Chimichurri Mayo:
- In a bowl, mix together mayonnaise, finely chopped parsley, finely chopped cilantro, minced garlic, red wine vinegar, dried oregano, salt, and black pepper to create the chimichurri mayo. Refrigerate until ready to use.

Prepare Caramelized Onions:
- In a skillet, caramelize the thinly sliced onions over medium heat until golden brown and sweet.

Grill the Bell Peppers:
- Grill the thinly sliced red bell peppers until they are tender with grill marks.

Toast the Rolls:
- Slice the Portuguese or crusty rolls in half and lightly toast them on the grill.

Assemble the Sandwich:
- Spread a generous amount of chimichurri mayo on the bottom half of each roll. Place the grilled Brazilian sausages on top.

Add Toppings:
- Layer with caramelized onions and grilled red bell peppers.

Finish Assembling:
- Place the top half of the roll on the assembled ingredients, creating a sandwich.

Serve:
- Serve the Brazilian Sausage Sandwich hot, accompanied by your favorite side dishes or a refreshing salad.

Enjoy:
- Enjoy the flavorful and hearty Brazilian Sausage Sandwich with the zesty kick of chimichurri mayo, capturing the essence of Brazilian cuisine.

Spicy Grilled Shrimp Skewers

Ingredients:

For the Marinade:

- 1 pound large shrimp, peeled and deveined
- 3 tablespoons olive oil
- 2 tablespoons fresh lime juice
- 2 cloves garlic, minced
- 1 teaspoon smoked paprika
- 1 teaspoon ground cumin
- 1 teaspoon chili powder
- 1/2 teaspoon cayenne pepper (adjust to taste)
- Salt and black pepper to taste

For the Skewers:

- Wooden or metal skewers
- Fresh cilantro, chopped (for garnish)
- Lime wedges (for serving)

Instructions:

Prepare the Shrimp:
- If using wooden skewers, soak them in water for about 30 minutes to prevent burning on the grill. Pat the shrimp dry with paper towels.

Make the Marinade:
- In a bowl, whisk together olive oil, fresh lime juice, minced garlic, smoked paprika, ground cumin, chili powder, cayenne pepper, salt, and black pepper to create the marinade.

Marinate the Shrimp:
- Place the shrimp in a shallow dish and pour the marinade over them. Toss the shrimp to coat evenly. Marinate for 15-30 minutes in the refrigerator.

Preheat the Grill:
- Preheat your grill to medium-high heat.

Skewer the Shrimp:
- Thread the marinated shrimp onto skewers, leaving space between each shrimp.

Grill the Skewers:
- Place the shrimp skewers on the preheated grill. Grill for about 2-3 minutes per side or until the shrimp are opaque and have grill marks.

Check for Doneness:
- Ensure the shrimp are cooked through but not overcooked. They should be opaque with a slight char.

Remove from Grill:
- Once cooked, remove the shrimp skewers from the grill.

Garnish:
- Sprinkle chopped fresh cilantro over the grilled shrimp.

Serve:
- Serve the Spicy Grilled Shrimp Skewers hot with lime wedges on the side for squeezing.

Enjoy:
- Enjoy these flavorful and spicy grilled shrimp skewers as a delicious appetizer or main dish, perfect for summer gatherings or as a quick weeknight meal.

Churrasco Pork Belly

Ingredients:

For the Pork Belly:

- 2 pounds pork belly, skin-on
- 3 cloves garlic, minced
- 2 tablespoons olive oil
- 2 tablespoons fresh lime juice
- 1 tablespoon smoked paprika
- 1 tablespoon ground cumin
- 1 tablespoon brown sugar
- 1 teaspoon dried oregano
- Salt and black pepper to taste

For the Chimichurri Sauce:

- 1 cup fresh parsley, finely chopped
- 1/4 cup fresh cilantro, finely chopped
- 3 cloves garlic, minced
- 1/2 cup extra-virgin olive oil
- 2 tablespoons red wine vinegar
- 1 teaspoon dried oregano
- 1/2 teaspoon red pepper flakes (adjust to taste)
- Salt and black pepper to taste

Instructions:

Prepare the Pork Belly:
- If using wooden skewers, soak them in water for about 30 minutes to prevent burning on the grill. Pat the pork belly dry with paper towels.

Make the Marinade:
- In a bowl, whisk together minced garlic, olive oil, fresh lime juice, smoked paprika, ground cumin, brown sugar, dried oregano, salt, and black pepper to create the marinade.

Marinate the Pork Belly:
- Score the skin of the pork belly with a sharp knife. Place the pork belly in a shallow dish, and rub the marinade all over the meat, making sure to get it

into the scores on the skin. Marinate for at least 2 hours or, preferably, overnight in the refrigerator.

Preheat the Grill:
- Preheat your grill to medium-high heat.

Grill the Pork Belly:
- Remove the pork belly from the marinade and let excess marinade drip off. Place the pork belly, skin side down, on the preheated grill. Grill for about 15-20 minutes, turning occasionally, until the skin is crispy, and the meat is cooked through.

Make the Chimichurri Sauce:
- While the pork belly is grilling, prepare the chimichurri sauce. In a bowl, mix together finely chopped parsley, finely chopped cilantro, minced garlic, extra-virgin olive oil, red wine vinegar, dried oregano, red pepper flakes, salt, and black pepper.

Slice and Serve:
- Once the pork belly is cooked, remove it from the grill and let it rest for a few minutes. Slice it into thick pieces.

Drizzle with Chimichurri:
- Drizzle the churrasco pork belly slices with the prepared chimichurri sauce.

Garnish and Enjoy:
- Garnish with additional fresh herbs if desired. Serve the Churrasco Pork Belly hot and enjoy the rich and flavorful taste of Brazilian churrasco.

Brazilian Garlic Butter Bread

Ingredients:

For the Garlic Butter:

- 1 cup (2 sticks) unsalted butter, softened
- 6 cloves garlic, minced
- 1/4 cup fresh parsley, finely chopped
- 1 teaspoon paprika
- Salt to taste

For the Bread:

- 4 large French bread or baguette loaves, cut into halves lengthwise

Instructions:

Prepare the Garlic Butter:
- In a bowl, combine softened butter, minced garlic, finely chopped fresh parsley, paprika, and salt. Mix until well combined. Adjust the salt to your taste.

Slice the Bread:
- Cut the French bread or baguette loaves into halves lengthwise, creating flat surfaces for spreading the garlic butter.

Spread the Garlic Butter:
- Generously spread the garlic butter mixture over the cut surfaces of the bread, ensuring even coverage.

Wrap in Foil:
- Wrap each garlic butter-coated bread half in aluminum foil, creating individual packets.

Preheat the Grill:
- Preheat your grill to medium heat.

Grill the Garlic Bread:
- Place the foil-wrapped garlic bread on the preheated grill. Grill for about 10-15 minutes, turning occasionally, until the bread is toasted and the garlic butter has melted into the bread.

Serve:

- Remove the garlic bread from the grill and carefully unwrap the foil. Slice the garlic butter bread into individual servings.

Garnish (Optional):
- Garnish with additional chopped parsley if desired.

Enjoy:
- Serve the Brazilian Garlic Butter Bread hot as a flavorful and aromatic side dish, perfect for accompanying grilled meats or as a delicious appetizer.

Brazilian Skirt Steak

Ingredients:

For the Steak:

- 2 pounds skirt steak or picanha
- Coarse salt (rock salt) for seasoning

For the Chimichurri Sauce:

- 1 cup fresh parsley, finely chopped
- 1/4 cup fresh cilantro, finely chopped
- 3 cloves garlic, minced
- 1/2 cup extra-virgin olive oil
- 2 tablespoons red wine vinegar
- 1 teaspoon dried oregano
- 1/2 teaspoon red pepper flakes (adjust to taste)
- Salt and black pepper to taste

Instructions:

Prepare the Chimichurri Sauce:
- In a bowl, mix together finely chopped parsley, finely chopped cilantro, minced garlic, extra-virgin olive oil, red wine vinegar, dried oregano, red pepper flakes, salt, and black pepper. Set aside to allow the flavors to meld.

Prepare the Skirt Steak:
- If using skirt steak, trim excess fat. If using picanha, ensure it is properly trimmed and scored. Score the meat's surface lightly with a sharp knife.

Season with Salt:
- Generously season the skirt steak or picanha with coarse salt, pressing it into the meat. Let it sit for at least 30 minutes to allow the salt to penetrate.

Preheat the Grill:
- Preheat your grill to high heat.

Grill the Steak:

- Place the skirt steak or picanha on the preheated grill. Grill for about 3-5 minutes per side, depending on the thickness and desired level of doneness.

Check for Doneness:
- Skirt steak is best served medium-rare to medium. Picanha can be cooked to medium-rare, medium, or medium-well based on preference.

Rest the Steak:
- Once cooked, remove the steak from the grill and let it rest for a few minutes.

Slice and Serve:
- Slice the skirt steak against the grain into thin strips. For picanha, slice it into thicker pieces.

Serve with Chimichurri Sauce:
- Serve the grilled Brazilian skirt steak or picanha with the prepared chimichurri sauce on the side for dipping or drizzling.

Enjoy:
- Enjoy the delicious and flavorful Brazilian Skirt Steak, a classic churrasco dish, served with the vibrant and herby chimichurri sauce.

Grilled Eggplant with Chimichurri

Ingredients:

For the Grilled Eggplant:

- 2 large eggplants, sliced into 1/2-inch rounds
- 2 tablespoons olive oil
- Salt and black pepper to taste

For the Chimichurri Sauce:

- 1 cup fresh parsley, finely chopped
- 1/4 cup fresh cilantro, finely chopped
- 3 cloves garlic, minced
- 1/2 cup extra-virgin olive oil
- 2 tablespoons red wine vinegar
- 1 teaspoon dried oregano
- 1/2 teaspoon red pepper flakes (adjust to taste)
- Salt and black pepper to taste

Instructions:

Prepare the Chimichurri Sauce:
- In a bowl, combine finely chopped parsley, finely chopped cilantro, minced garlic, extra-virgin olive oil, red wine vinegar, dried oregano, red pepper flakes, salt, and black pepper. Set aside to allow the flavors to meld.

Preheat the Grill:
- Preheat your grill to medium-high heat.

Prepare the Eggplant:
- Slice the eggplants into 1/2-inch rounds. Brush both sides of each slice with olive oil and season with salt and black pepper.

Grill the Eggplant:
- Place the eggplant slices on the preheated grill. Grill for about 3-4 minutes per side, or until they are tender and have grill marks.

Check for Doneness:

- Ensure the eggplant is cooked through and has a nice smoky flavor from the grill.

Arrange on a Platter:
- Arrange the grilled eggplant slices on a serving platter.

Serve with Chimichurri:
- Drizzle the prepared chimichurri sauce over the grilled eggplant or serve it on the side for dipping.

Garnish (Optional):
- Garnish with additional chopped herbs if desired.

Enjoy:
- Enjoy the Grilled Eggplant with Chimichurri Sauce as a flavorful and vibrant side dish, perfect for summer grilling or as part of a vegetarian meal.

Brazilian Smoked Sausage

Ingredients:

For the Smoked Sausage:

- 1 pound Brazilian smoked sausage (linguiça calabresa), sliced into rounds

For the Marinade:

- 2 tablespoons olive oil
- 2 cloves garlic, minced
- 1 tablespoon sweet paprika
- 1 teaspoon dried oregano
- 1 teaspoon cayenne pepper (adjust to taste)
- Salt and black pepper to taste

Instructions:

Prepare the Marinade:
- In a bowl, mix together olive oil, minced garlic, sweet paprika, dried oregano, cayenne pepper, salt, and black pepper to create the marinade.

Slice the Smoked Sausage:
- Slice the Brazilian smoked sausage (linguiça calabresa) into rounds, about 1/2-inch thick.

Marinate the Sausage:
- Place the sliced sausage in a bowl, and toss it with the prepared marinade. Ensure each slice is well coated. Let it marinate for at least 30 minutes to allow the flavors to infuse.

Preheat the Grill:
- Preheat your grill to medium-high heat.

Skewer the Sausage:
- Thread the marinated sausage rounds onto skewers, leaving space between each piece.

Grill the Sausage Skewers:

- Place the sausage skewers on the preheated grill. Grill for about 10-15 minutes, turning occasionally, until the sausage is cooked through and has a nice smoky flavor.

Check for Doneness:
- Ensure the sausage is browned and cooked to your liking.

Serve:
- Remove the smoked sausage skewers from the grill and arrange them on a serving platter.

Enjoy:
- Enjoy the Brazilian Smoked Sausage hot off the grill as a flavorful appetizer, snack, or as part of a larger churrasco-style feast.

Brazilian Grilled Portobello Mushrooms

Ingredients:

For the Grilled Portobello Mushrooms:

- 4 large portobello mushrooms, stems removed
- 3 tablespoons olive oil
- 2 tablespoons balsamic vinegar
- 2 cloves garlic, minced
- 1 teaspoon dried thyme
- Salt and black pepper to taste

For the Chimichurri Sauce:

- 1 cup fresh parsley, finely chopped
- 1/4 cup fresh cilantro, finely chopped
- 3 cloves garlic, minced
- 1/2 cup extra-virgin olive oil
- 2 tablespoons red wine vinegar
- 1 teaspoon dried oregano
- 1/2 teaspoon red pepper flakes (adjust to taste)
- Salt and black pepper to taste

Instructions:

Prepare the Chimichurri Sauce:
- In a bowl, combine finely chopped parsley, finely chopped cilantro, minced garlic, extra-virgin olive oil, red wine vinegar, dried oregano, red pepper flakes, salt, and black pepper. Set aside to allow the flavors to meld.

Prepare the Portobello Mushrooms:
- Clean the portobello mushrooms and remove the stems. Place them in a shallow dish.

Make the Marinade:
- In a small bowl, whisk together olive oil, balsamic vinegar, minced garlic, dried thyme, salt, and black pepper.

Marinate the Mushrooms:

- Brush the portobello mushrooms with the prepared marinade, ensuring they are well coated on both sides. Let them marinate for at least 20-30 minutes.

Preheat the Grill:
- Preheat your grill to medium-high heat.

Grill the Portobello Mushrooms:
- Place the marinated portobello mushrooms on the preheated grill. Grill for about 5-7 minutes per side, or until they are tender and have grill marks.

Check for Doneness:
- Ensure the mushrooms are cooked through and have a nice smoky flavor from the grill.

Serve:
- Arrange the grilled portobello mushrooms on a serving platter.

Drizzle with Chimichurri:
- Drizzle the prepared chimichurri sauce over the grilled portobello mushrooms or serve it on the side for dipping.

Garnish (Optional):
- Garnish with additional chopped herbs if desired.

Enjoy:
- Enjoy the Brazilian Grilled Portobello Mushrooms as a delicious and savory side dish or as a vegetarian option for a churrasco-style meal.

Brazilian Garlic-Lime Chicken Drumsticks

Ingredients:

For the Chicken Marinade:

- 2 pounds chicken drumsticks
- 4 cloves garlic, minced
- 1/4 cup fresh lime juice
- 2 tablespoons olive oil
- 1 tablespoon sweet paprika
- 1 teaspoon dried oregano
- 1 teaspoon ground cumin
- 1 teaspoon onion powder
- 1 teaspoon brown sugar
- Salt and black pepper to taste

For the Garlic-Lime Glaze:

- 2 tablespoons butter
- 3 cloves garlic, minced
- Zest of 1 lime
- 1 tablespoon fresh lime juice
- 1 tablespoon chopped fresh parsley (for garnish)
- Salt and black pepper to taste

Instructions:

Prepare the Chicken Drumsticks:
- Clean and pat dry the chicken drumsticks.

Make the Chicken Marinade:
- In a bowl, combine minced garlic, fresh lime juice, olive oil, sweet paprika, dried oregano, ground cumin, onion powder, brown sugar, salt, and black pepper to create the marinade.

Marinate the Chicken:
- Place the chicken drumsticks in a shallow dish and rub them with the prepared marinade. Ensure each drumstick is well coated. Marinate for at least 2 hours, or preferably, overnight in the refrigerator.

Preheat the Grill:

- Preheat your grill to medium-high heat.

Grill the Chicken Drumsticks:
- Place the marinated chicken drumsticks on the preheated grill. Grill for about 20-25 minutes, turning occasionally, until the chicken is cooked through, and the skin is crispy and charred.

Make the Garlic-Lime Glaze:
- In a small saucepan, melt the butter over medium heat. Add minced garlic and sauté until fragrant. Stir in the lime zest and lime juice. Season with salt and black pepper. Cook for an additional 2-3 minutes until the glaze thickens slightly.

Brush with Glaze:
- Brush the grilled chicken drumsticks with the garlic-lime glaze during the last 5 minutes of grilling, ensuring they are well coated.

Check for Doneness:
- Ensure the chicken drumsticks are cooked through with an internal temperature of 165°F (74°C).

Garnish and Serve:
- Transfer the grilled chicken drumsticks to a serving platter. Drizzle any remaining glaze over the top and garnish with chopped fresh parsley.

Enjoy:
- Serve the Brazilian Garlic-Lime Chicken Drumsticks hot and enjoy the flavorful combination of garlic, lime, and spices. Perfect for a Brazilian-inspired barbecue feast!

Cachaça-Glazed Grilled Pineapple

Ingredients:

For the Cachaça Glaze:

- 1/2 cup cachaça (Brazilian sugarcane spirit)
- 1/2 cup brown sugar
- 1/4 cup unsalted butter
- 1 teaspoon vanilla extract

For the Grilled Pineapple:

- 1 large pineapple, peeled, cored, and cut into rings or spears

Instructions:

Prepare the Cachaça Glaze:
- In a small saucepan over medium heat, combine cachaça, brown sugar, unsalted butter, and vanilla extract. Stir until the sugar is dissolved, and the mixture is well combined.

Simmer the Glaze:
- Bring the mixture to a simmer, then reduce the heat to low. Allow the glaze to simmer for 8-10 minutes, or until it thickens slightly. Remove from heat and let it cool.

Preheat the Grill:
- Preheat your grill to medium-high heat.

Grill the Pineapple:
- Place the pineapple rings or spears on the preheated grill. Grill for about 2-3 minutes per side, or until the pineapple has grill marks and is slightly caramelized.

Brush with Cachaça Glaze:
- Brush the grilled pineapple with the cachaça glaze during the last minute of grilling, ensuring each piece is well coated.

Check for Caramelization:
- Ensure the pineapple is caramelized to your liking, with a slightly golden-brown color.

Remove from Grill:

- Remove the grilled pineapple from the grill and place it on a serving platter.

Drizzle with Glaze:
- Drizzle any remaining cachaça glaze over the grilled pineapple for an extra burst of flavor.

Serve:
- Serve the Cachaça-Glazed Grilled Pineapple as a delightful and boozy dessert or side dish. It's perfect for a Brazilian-inspired barbecue or a sweet treat on its own.

Enjoy:
- Enjoy the unique combination of cachaça-infused glaze and grilled pineapple, creating a delicious and tropical flavor experience.

Brazilian Garlic-Lime Butter Steak

Ingredients:

For the Steak:

- 4 ribeye steaks or your preferred cut (about 1 inch thick)
- Salt and black pepper to taste
- Olive oil for brushing

For the Garlic-Lime Butter:

- 1/2 cup unsalted butter, softened
- 4 cloves garlic, minced
- Zest of 2 limes
- 2 tablespoons fresh lime juice
- 1 tablespoon chopped fresh parsley
- Salt and black pepper to taste

Instructions:

Prepare the Steak:
- Take the ribeye steaks out of the refrigerator and let them come to room temperature for about 30 minutes. Pat them dry with paper towels and season both sides with salt and black pepper.

Preheat the Grill:
- Preheat your grill to high heat.

Brush with Olive Oil:
- Brush both sides of the steaks with olive oil to prevent sticking on the grill.

Grill the Steaks:
- Place the steaks on the preheated grill. Grill for about 4-5 minutes per side for medium-rare, adjusting the time based on your preferred level of doneness.

Check for Doneness:
- Use a meat thermometer to check the internal temperature. For medium-rare, it should be around 130°F (54°C).

Rest the Steaks:

- Once cooked to your liking, remove the steaks from the grill and let them rest for a few minutes.

Prepare the Garlic-Lime Butter:
- While the steaks are resting, prepare the garlic-lime butter. In a bowl, combine softened butter, minced garlic, lime zest, lime juice, chopped fresh parsley, salt, and black pepper. Mix until well combined.

Slice and Serve:
- Slice the rested steaks against the grain into thin strips.

Top with Garlic-Lime Butter:
- Place a generous dollop of the garlic-lime butter on top of each steak slice.

Garnish (Optional):
- Garnish with additional chopped parsley and lime wedges if desired.

Enjoy:
- Serve the Brazilian Garlic-Lime Butter Steak hot and savor the combination of savory steak and zesty, herby butter. It's a delightful burst of flavors reminiscent of Brazilian churrasco.

Churrasco Picanha Burger

Ingredients:

For the Picanha Patties:

- 1 pound ground beef (preferably picanha cut)
- Salt and black pepper to taste

For the Chimichurri Mayo:

- 1/2 cup mayonnaise
- 2 tablespoons fresh parsley, finely chopped
- 1 tablespoon fresh cilantro, finely chopped
- 2 cloves garlic, minced
- 1 tablespoon red wine vinegar
- 1/4 cup extra-virgin olive oil
- Salt and black pepper to taste

For Assembling:

- Burger buns
- Lettuce leaves
- Sliced tomatoes
- Sliced red onions

Instructions:

Prepare the Picanha Patties:
- In a bowl, gently mix the ground beef with salt and black pepper. Form the mixture into burger patties, ensuring they are loosely packed for a juicy texture.

Preheat the Grill:
- Preheat your grill to medium-high heat.

Grill the Picanha Patties:
- Place the picanha patties on the preheated grill. Grill for about 4-5 minutes per side, or until they reach your preferred level of doneness.

Check for Doneness:
- Use a meat thermometer to check the internal temperature of the patties. For medium-rare, it should be around 130°F (54°C).

Rest the Patties:
- Once cooked, remove the picanha patties from the grill and let them rest for a few minutes.

Prepare the Chimichurri Mayo:
- In a bowl, mix together mayonnaise, finely chopped parsley, finely chopped cilantro, minced garlic, red wine vinegar, extra-virgin olive oil, salt, and black pepper. Set aside.

Assemble the Burgers:
- Toast the burger buns on the grill if desired. Place a lettuce leaf on the bottom half of each bun.

Add the Picanha Patties:
- Place the grilled picanha patties on top of the lettuce.

Layer with Toppings:
- Add sliced tomatoes and red onions on top of the patties.

Drizzle with Chimichurri Mayo:
- Generously drizzle the chimichurri mayo over the toppings.

Complete the Burger:
- Top with the other half of the burger bun.

Serve:
- Serve the Churrasco Picanha Burger hot, and enjoy the delicious fusion of traditional churrasco flavors in a burger form.

Enjoy:
- Bite into the juicy and flavorful Churrasco Picanha Burger for a tasty Brazilian-inspired treat!

Brazilian Lemon-Garlic Swordfish

Ingredients:

For the Swordfish:

- 4 swordfish steaks
- Salt and black pepper to taste
- 2 tablespoons olive oil

For the Lemon-Garlic Marinade:

- 1/4 cup olive oil
- Zest of 2 lemons
- Juice of 2 lemons
- 4 cloves garlic, minced
- 1 tablespoon fresh parsley, chopped
- 1 teaspoon dried oregano
- Salt and black pepper to taste

Instructions:

Prepare the Lemon-Garlic Marinade:
- In a bowl, whisk together olive oil, lemon zest, lemon juice, minced garlic, chopped fresh parsley, dried oregano, salt, and black pepper to create the marinade.

Marinate the Swordfish:
- Place the swordfish steaks in a shallow dish. Pour the lemon-garlic marinade over the swordfish, ensuring each steak is well coated. Marinate for at least 30 minutes, allowing the flavors to infuse.

Preheat the Grill:
- Preheat your grill to medium-high heat.

Season the Swordfish:
- Remove the swordfish from the marinade and season both sides with salt and black pepper. Drizzle the swordfish steaks with olive oil.

Grill the Swordfish:

- Place the swordfish steaks on the preheated grill. Grill for about 3-4 minutes per side, or until the fish is cooked through and has grill marks.

Check for Doneness:
- The swordfish should be opaque and flake easily with a fork. The internal temperature should reach 145°F (63°C).

Remove from Grill:
- Once cooked, remove the swordfish steaks from the grill and let them rest for a few minutes.

Serve:
- Transfer the grilled swordfish to a serving platter.

Garnish (Optional):
- Garnish with additional chopped parsley and lemon wedges if desired.

Enjoy:
- Serve the Brazilian Lemon-Garlic Swordfish hot and savor the bright and zesty flavors. This dish is perfect for a light and refreshing seafood meal with a Brazilian twist.

Brazilian BBQ Chicken Skewers

Ingredients:

For the Chicken Skewers:

- 2 pounds boneless, skinless chicken thighs, cut into bite-sized pieces
- 2 tablespoons olive oil
- 2 cloves garlic, minced
- 1 teaspoon smoked paprika
- 1 teaspoon ground cumin
- 1 teaspoon dried oregano
- Salt and black pepper to taste
- Wooden skewers, soaked in water for at least 30 minutes

For the Chimichurri Sauce:

- 1 cup fresh parsley, finely chopped
- 1/4 cup fresh cilantro, finely chopped
- 3 cloves garlic, minced
- 1/2 cup extra-virgin olive oil
- 2 tablespoons red wine vinegar
- 1 teaspoon dried oregano
- 1/2 teaspoon red pepper flakes (adjust to taste)
- Salt and black pepper to taste

Instructions:

Prepare the Chicken Skewers:
- In a bowl, combine olive oil, minced garlic, smoked paprika, ground cumin, dried oregano, salt, and black pepper. Add the chicken pieces and toss to coat evenly. Let it marinate for at least 30 minutes, or preferably, overnight in the refrigerator.

Preheat the Grill:
- Preheat your grill to medium-high heat.

Skewer the Chicken:
- Thread the marinated chicken pieces onto the soaked wooden skewers.

Grill the Chicken Skewers:
- Place the chicken skewers on the preheated grill. Grill for about 5-7 minutes per side, or until the chicken is cooked through and has a nice char.

Check for Doneness:
- Ensure the chicken reaches an internal temperature of 165°F (74°C).

Prepare the Chimichurri Sauce:
- In a bowl, combine finely chopped parsley, finely chopped cilantro, minced garlic, extra-virgin olive oil, red wine vinegar, dried oregano, red pepper flakes, salt, and black pepper. Set aside.

Serve:
- Arrange the grilled chicken skewers on a serving platter.

Drizzle with Chimichurri:
- Drizzle the prepared chimichurri sauce over the chicken skewers or serve it on the side for dipping.

Garnish (Optional):
- Garnish with additional chopped herbs if desired.

Enjoy:
- Serve the Brazilian BBQ Chicken Skewers hot and enjoy the smoky, flavorful taste with the vibrant chimichurri sauce. Perfect for a Brazilian-inspired barbecue feast!

Grilled Beef Heart

Ingredients:

For the Marinade:

- 1 beef heart, cleaned and trimmed
- 1/2 cup olive oil
- 1/4 cup red wine vinegar
- 4 cloves garlic, minced
- 1 teaspoon smoked paprika
- 1 teaspoon ground cumin
- 1 teaspoon dried oregano
- Salt and black pepper to taste

Instructions:

Prepare the Beef Heart:
- Clean and trim the beef heart, removing excess fat and connective tissue. Cut the heart into manageable pieces.

Make the Marinade:
- In a bowl, whisk together olive oil, red wine vinegar, minced garlic, smoked paprika, ground cumin, dried oregano, salt, and black pepper to create the marinade.

Marinate the Beef Heart:
- Place the beef heart pieces in a shallow dish, and pour the marinade over them. Ensure the pieces are well coated. Cover and refrigerate for at least 4 hours or overnight for the flavors to infuse.

Preheat the Grill:
- Preheat your grill to medium-high heat.

Skewer the Beef Heart:
- Thread the marinated beef heart pieces onto skewers for easy grilling.

Grill the Beef Heart:
- Place the skewered beef heart on the preheated grill. Grill for about 4-5 minutes per side, or until the beef heart is cooked through and has a nice char.

Check for Doneness:

- Ensure the beef heart reaches an internal temperature of at least 145°F (63°C).

Rest and Slice:
- Remove the beef heart from the grill and let it rest for a few minutes. Slice the beef heart into thin pieces.

Serve:
- Arrange the grilled beef heart slices on a serving platter.

Garnish (Optional):
- Garnish with fresh herbs or a squeeze of lemon if desired.

Enjoy:
- Serve the Grilled Beef Heart slices hot and savor the unique and hearty flavor. This dish is a delicacy in many cultures and is a delicious addition to a barbecue or special meal.

Brazilian Grilled Cheese with Guava Paste

Ingredients:

- Sliced Brazilian cheese (common choices include Queijo Minas or Queijo Coalho)
- Guava paste (Goiabada), sliced
- Butter for grilling

Instructions:

Preheat the Grill or Pan:
- Preheat a grill or a pan over medium heat.

Butter the Cheese:
- Lightly butter one side of each slice of Brazilian cheese.

Assemble the Sandwich:
- Place a slice of guava paste on the unbuttered side of one cheese slice. Top it with another cheese slice, buttered side facing out, to create a sandwich.

Grill the Sandwich:
- Place the assembled sandwich on the preheated grill or pan. Grill for about 2-3 minutes per side, or until the cheese is melted, and the bread is golden brown.

Check for Melting:
- Press the sandwich gently with a spatula to ensure the cheese and guava paste are melting together.

Remove from Heat:
- Once the sandwich is grilled to perfection, remove it from the heat.

Slice and Serve:
- Allow the sandwich to cool for a moment, then slice it into halves or quarters.

Enjoy:
- Serve the Brazilian Grilled Cheese with Guava Paste warm and enjoy the delightful combination of gooey melted cheese and sweet guava paste. This is a popular Brazilian snack known for its unique and delicious flavor profile.

Crispy Brazilian Pork Belly Skewers

Ingredients:

For the Pork Belly:

- 2 pounds pork belly, skin-on, cut into bite-sized cubes
- 2 tablespoons olive oil
- 1 tablespoon paprika
- 1 tablespoon ground cumin
- 1 tablespoon garlic powder
- 1 tablespoon onion powder
- 1 teaspoon cayenne pepper (adjust to taste)
- Salt and black pepper to taste

For the Skewers:

- Wooden skewers, soaked in water for at least 30 minutes

Instructions:

Prepare the Pork Belly:
- Pat the pork belly cubes dry with paper towels. Score the skin side with a sharp knife, making shallow cuts.

Marinate the Pork Belly:
- In a bowl, combine olive oil, paprika, ground cumin, garlic powder, onion powder, cayenne pepper, salt, and black pepper. Mix well to create the marinade. Coat the pork belly cubes with the marinade, ensuring they are well covered. Marinate for at least 2 hours or overnight in the refrigerator.

Preheat the Grill:
- Preheat your grill to medium-high heat.

Skewer the Pork Belly:
- Thread the marinated pork belly cubes onto the soaked wooden skewers.

Grill the Skewers:
- Place the skewers on the preheated grill. Grill for about 10-15 minutes, turning occasionally, or until the pork belly is cooked through and has a crispy skin.

Check for Doneness:
- Ensure the pork belly reaches an internal temperature of at least 145°F (63°C) and that the skin is crispy.

Remove from Grill:
- Once cooked, remove the skewers from the grill.

Rest and Slice:
- Let the skewers rest for a few minutes before slicing the pork belly into bite-sized pieces.

Serve:
- Arrange the Crispy Brazilian Pork Belly Skewers on a serving platter.

Garnish (Optional):
- Garnish with fresh herbs or serve with a dipping sauce of your choice.

Enjoy:
- Serve the Crispy Brazilian Pork Belly Skewers hot and enjoy the irresistible combination of crispy skin and flavorful, tender pork belly. This dish is perfect for a Brazilian barbecue or as a delicious appetizer.

Brazilian Grilled Zucchini

Ingredients:

- 4 medium-sized zucchini, sliced into rounds or spears
- 2 tablespoons olive oil
- 2 cloves garlic, minced
- 1 tablespoon fresh parsley, chopped
- 1 teaspoon ground cumin
- Salt and black pepper to taste
- Lemon wedges for serving (optional)

Instructions:

Preheat the Grill:
- Preheat your grill to medium-high heat.

Prepare the Zucchini:
- Slice the zucchini into rounds or spears, depending on your preference.

Make the Marinade:
- In a bowl, mix together olive oil, minced garlic, chopped fresh parsley, ground cumin, salt, and black pepper to create a simple marinade.

Marinate the Zucchini:
- Toss the zucchini slices in the marinade, ensuring they are well coated.

Grill the Zucchini:
- Place the marinated zucchini on the preheated grill. Grill for about 3-5 minutes per side, or until the zucchini is tender and has grill marks.

Check for Doneness:
- Pierce the zucchini with a fork to check for tenderness. It should be cooked but still have a slight crunch.

Remove from Grill:
- Once cooked, remove the grilled zucchini from the grill.

Serve:
- Arrange the Grilled Zucchini on a serving platter.

Garnish (Optional):
- Garnish with additional chopped parsley and serve with lemon wedges if desired.

Enjoy:

- Serve the Brazilian Grilled Zucchini as a flavorful and healthy side dish. The combination of grilled zucchini with garlic and cumin creates a delicious and aromatic accompaniment to any Brazilian-inspired meal.

Churrasco Lamb Leg

Ingredients:

For the Marinade:

- 1 leg of lamb (approximately 5-6 pounds)
- 1/2 cup olive oil
- 1/4 cup red wine vinegar
- 4 cloves garlic, minced
- 2 tablespoons fresh rosemary, chopped
- 1 tablespoon fresh thyme, chopped
- 1 tablespoon paprika
- 1 teaspoon cayenne pepper (adjust to taste)
- Salt and black pepper to taste

For Grilling:

- Charcoal or gas grill

Instructions:

Prepare the Marinade:
- In a bowl, combine olive oil, red wine vinegar, minced garlic, chopped rosemary, chopped thyme, paprika, cayenne pepper, salt, and black pepper. Mix well to create the marinade.

Prepare the Lamb Leg:
- Place the lamb leg in a large dish or a resealable plastic bag. Score the surface of the lamb leg with a sharp knife, creating small incisions for the marinade to penetrate.

Marinate the Lamb:
- Pour the marinade over the lamb leg, ensuring it is well-coated. Massage the marinade into the meat, covering it thoroughly. Marinate for at least 4 hours, or preferably, overnight in the refrigerator.

Preheat the Grill:
- Preheat your charcoal or gas grill to medium-high heat.

Prepare the Lamb for Grilling:
- Remove the lamb leg from the marinade and let it come to room temperature for about 30 minutes.

Grill the Lamb Leg:
- Place the lamb leg on the preheated grill. Grill for approximately 15-20 minutes per side, depending on the desired level of doneness. Use a meat thermometer to check the internal temperature (145°F/63°C for medium-rare, 160°F/71°C for medium).

Baste with Marinade (Optional):
- Optionally, baste the lamb leg with some of the remaining marinade during the grilling process for added flavor.

Rest and Carve:
- Once cooked to your liking, remove the lamb leg from the grill and let it rest for about 10 minutes. This allows the juices to redistribute.

Carve and Serve:
- Carve the Churrasco Lamb Leg into slices and serve on a platter.

Enjoy:
- Serve the Churrasco Lamb Leg hot and enjoy the succulent and flavorful taste of grilled lamb with aromatic herbs. This dish is a fantastic centerpiece for a Brazilian-inspired barbecue.

Brazilian Herb-Marinated Tofu Skewers

Ingredients:

For the Marinade:

- 1 block firm tofu, pressed and cubed
- 1/4 cup olive oil
- 2 tablespoons soy sauce or tamari
- 2 tablespoons lime juice
- 4 cloves garlic, minced
- 2 tablespoons fresh cilantro, chopped
- 1 tablespoon fresh parsley, chopped
- 1 teaspoon ground cumin
- 1 teaspoon smoked paprika
- 1 teaspoon agave nectar or maple syrup
- Salt and black pepper to taste

For Skewering:

- Wooden skewers, soaked in water for at least 30 minutes

Instructions:

Prepare the Marinade:
- In a bowl, whisk together olive oil, soy sauce or tamari, lime juice, minced garlic, chopped cilantro, chopped parsley, ground cumin, smoked paprika, agave nectar or maple syrup, salt, and black pepper.

Prepare the Tofu:
- Press the tofu to remove excess water and cut it into bite-sized cubes.

Marinate the Tofu:
- Place the tofu cubes in a shallow dish and pour the marinade over them. Ensure the tofu is well-coated. Marinate for at least 30 minutes, or longer for enhanced flavor.

Skewer the Tofu:
- Thread the marinated tofu cubes onto the soaked wooden skewers.

Preheat the Grill or Oven:

- Preheat your grill or oven to medium-high heat.

Grill or Bake the Skewers:
- Grill the tofu skewers for about 10-15 minutes, turning occasionally, or bake them in the oven at 400°F (200°C) for approximately 20-25 minutes. Cook until the tofu has a golden-brown exterior.

Check for Doneness:
- Ensure the tofu is cooked through and has a slightly crispy texture on the outside.

Remove from Heat:
- Once cooked, remove the skewers from the grill or oven.

Serve:
- Arrange the Brazilian Herb-Marinated Tofu Skewers on a serving platter.

Garnish (Optional):
- Garnish with additional fresh herbs and lime wedges if desired.

Enjoy:
- Serve the Tofu Skewers hot and savor the Brazilian-inspired herb-marinated flavor. This dish is a delightful and plant-based addition to any barbecue or meal.

Grilled Brazilian Halloumi

Ingredients:

- 1 block of halloumi cheese, sliced into 1/2-inch thick pieces
- 2 tablespoons olive oil
- 1 tablespoon fresh oregano, chopped
- 1 tablespoon fresh parsley, chopped
- 1 teaspoon smoked paprika
- 1 teaspoon cayenne pepper (adjust to taste)
- Zest of 1 lemon
- Salt and black pepper to taste
- Lemon wedges for serving

Instructions:

Preheat the Grill:
- Preheat your grill to medium-high heat.

Prepare the Halloumi:
- Slice the halloumi cheese into 1/2-inch thick pieces. Pat them dry with a paper towel.

Make the Marinade:
- In a bowl, combine olive oil, chopped oregano, chopped parsley, smoked paprika, cayenne pepper, lemon zest, salt, and black pepper. Mix well to create the marinade.

Marinate the Halloumi:
- Brush the halloumi slices with the marinade, ensuring they are well-coated on both sides. Allow them to marinate for about 15-20 minutes.

Grill the Halloumi:
- Place the marinated halloumi slices on the preheated grill. Grill for about 2-3 minutes per side, or until the cheese has grill marks and a golden-brown color.

Check for Doneness:
- The halloumi should be slightly crispy on the outside while remaining soft and gooey on the inside.

Remove from Grill:
- Once grilled to perfection, remove the halloumi slices from the grill.

Serve:

- Arrange the Grilled Brazilian Halloumi on a serving platter.

Garnish (Optional):
- Garnish with additional fresh herbs and serve with lemon wedges on the side.

Enjoy:
- Serve the Grilled Brazilian Halloumi hot and enjoy the smoky flavor and unique texture of this grilled cheese. This dish makes for a delightful appetizer or side for your Brazilian-inspired feast.

Brazilian Style Grilled Lobster Tails

Ingredients:

- 4 lobster tails, split in half lengthwise
- 1/2 cup olive oil
- 1/4 cup fresh cilantro, chopped
- 1/4 cup fresh parsley, chopped
- 4 cloves garlic, minced
- 2 tablespoons lime juice
- 1 teaspoon smoked paprika
- 1 teaspoon cayenne pepper (adjust to taste)
- Salt and black pepper to taste
- Lemon wedges for serving

Instructions:

Prepare the Lobster Tails:
- Use kitchen shears to cut the lobster tails in half lengthwise. Clean and devein the tails if needed.

Make the Marinade:
- In a bowl, combine olive oil, chopped cilantro, chopped parsley, minced garlic, lime juice, smoked paprika, cayenne pepper, salt, and black pepper. Mix well to create the marinade.

Marinate the Lobster Tails:
- Place the lobster tails in a shallow dish and brush the marinade over them, making sure each tail is well-coated. Allow them to marinate for at least 30 minutes.

Preheat the Grill:
- Preheat your grill to medium-high heat.

Grill the Lobster Tails:
- Place the marinated lobster tails on the preheated grill, cut side down. Grill for about 5-7 minutes, then flip and grill for an additional 5-7 minutes or until the lobster meat is opaque and has grill marks.

Baste with Marinade (Optional):
- Optionally, baste the lobster tails with some of the remaining marinade during the grilling process for added flavor.

Check for Doneness:

- Ensure the lobster meat is fully cooked, opaque, and easily pulls away from the shell.

Remove from Grill:
- Once grilled to perfection, remove the lobster tails from the grill.

Serve:
- Arrange the Grilled Brazilian Style Lobster Tails on a serving platter.

Garnish (Optional):
- Garnish with additional chopped herbs and serve with lemon wedges on the side.

Enjoy:
- Serve the Brazilian Style Grilled Lobster Tails hot and savor the rich and flavorful taste. This dish is perfect for a special occasion or as a luxurious addition to your Brazilian-inspired barbecue.

Churrasco-Style Grilled Okra

Ingredients:

- 1 pound fresh okra, ends trimmed
- 2 tablespoons olive oil
- 2 cloves garlic, minced
- 1 tablespoon fresh parsley, chopped
- 1 teaspoon smoked paprika
- 1 teaspoon ground cumin
- Salt and black pepper to taste
- Lemon wedges for serving

Instructions:

Prepare the Okra:
- Trim the ends of the fresh okra and rinse them under cold water. Pat them dry with a paper towel.

Make the Marinade:
- In a bowl, combine olive oil, minced garlic, chopped parsley, smoked paprika, ground cumin, salt, and black pepper. Mix well to create the marinade.

Marinate the Okra:
- Place the okra in a shallow dish and toss them with the marinade, ensuring they are well-coated. Allow them to marinate for at least 15-20 minutes.

Preheat the Grill:
- Preheat your grill to medium-high heat.

Grill the Okra:
- Place the marinated okra on the preheated grill. Grill for about 4-6 minutes, turning occasionally, or until the okra is tender and has grill marks.

Check for Doneness:
- Ensure the okra is cooked through and has a slightly charred exterior.

Remove from Grill:
- Once grilled to perfection, remove the okra from the grill.

Serve:
- Arrange the Churrasco-Style Grilled Okra on a serving platter.

Garnish (Optional):

- Garnish with additional chopped parsley and serve with lemon wedges on the side.

Enjoy:
- Serve the Churrasco-Style Grilled Okra hot and enjoy the smoky and flavorful taste. This dish is a delightful and unique way to prepare okra for a Brazilian-inspired barbecue or meal.

Brazilian BBQ Pulled Pork Sandwich

Ingredients:

For the Pulled Pork:

- 3 pounds pork shoulder or pork butt
- 2 tablespoons olive oil
- 1 large onion, finely chopped
- 4 cloves garlic, minced
- 1 cup Brazilian-style barbecue sauce (see recipe below)
- 1 cup chicken or vegetable broth
- Salt and black pepper to taste

For the Brazilian-Style Barbecue Sauce:

- 1 cup ketchup
- 1/2 cup apple cider vinegar
- 1/4 cup soy sauce
- 1/4 cup Worcestershire sauce
- 1/4 cup brown sugar
- 2 tablespoons Dijon mustard
- 1 tablespoon smoked paprika
- 1 teaspoon ground cumin
- 1 teaspoon chili powder
- Salt and black pepper to taste

For Assembling Sandwiches:

- Burger buns or rolls
- Coleslaw (optional)
- Pickles (optional)

Instructions:

Brazilian-Style Barbecue Sauce:

In a medium saucepan, combine all the barbecue sauce ingredients.
Bring the mixture to a simmer over medium heat, stirring frequently.
Simmer for about 10-15 minutes until the sauce thickens and flavors meld.
Adjust seasoning with salt and pepper as needed.
Set aside to cool.

Pulled Pork:

Preheat the oven to 325°F (163°C).
Season the pork shoulder with salt and black pepper.
In a large oven-safe pot or Dutch oven, heat olive oil over medium-high heat.
Brown the pork on all sides.
Add chopped onions and garlic to the pot and sauté until softened.
Pour in the Brazilian-style barbecue sauce and chicken or vegetable broth. Stir to combine.
Cover the pot and transfer it to the preheated oven. Roast for about 3-4 hours or until the pork is fork-tender and easily pulls apart.
Remove the pork from the pot and shred it using two forks. Place the shredded pork back into the pot and mix it with the sauce.
If needed, adjust the seasoning with salt and black pepper.

Assembling Sandwiches:

Toast the burger buns or rolls.
Spoon a generous portion of the Brazilian BBQ pulled pork onto the bottom half of each bun.
Top with coleslaw and pickles if desired.
Place the top half of the bun on the filling to create a sandwich.
Serve the Brazilian BBQ Pulled Pork Sandwiches hot and enjoy the delicious blend of flavors.

This sandwich is a delightful fusion of Brazilian barbecue flavors and classic pulled pork goodness.

Grilled Picanha Sandwich

Ingredients:

For the Picanha:

- 1.5 pounds picanha steak
- Salt and black pepper to taste

For the Chimichurri Sauce:

- 1 cup fresh parsley, chopped
- 1/4 cup fresh cilantro, chopped
- 4 cloves garlic, minced
- 1/2 cup olive oil
- 2 tablespoons red wine vinegar
- 1 teaspoon dried oregano
- 1/2 teaspoon red pepper flakes (optional)
- Salt and black pepper to taste

For the Sandwich:

- Baguette or your favorite bread, sliced
- Sliced tomatoes
- Sliced red onions
- Lettuce leaves
- Optional: Sliced cheese (such as provolone or Swiss)

Instructions:

Picanha:

Preheat the grill to medium-high heat.
Score the fat cap of the picanha in a diamond pattern. Season the entire steak generously with salt and black pepper.
Place the picanha on the preheated grill, fat side down, and cook for about 10-15 minutes or until the fat is crispy and rendered.

Flip the steak and continue grilling to your desired doneness. Picanha is typically served medium-rare to medium.

Remove the picanha from the grill and let it rest for a few minutes before slicing it against the grain into thin strips.

Chimichurri Sauce:

In a bowl, combine chopped parsley, chopped cilantro, minced garlic, olive oil, red wine vinegar, dried oregano, red pepper flakes (if using), salt, and black pepper. Mix well.

Adjust the seasoning to taste and set aside.

Assembling the Sandwich:

Slice the baguette or bread into sandwich-sized portions.

Spread a generous amount of chimichurri sauce on both sides of the bread.

Layer sliced picanha steak on the bottom half of the bread.

Top with sliced tomatoes, red onions, lettuce leaves, and optional sliced cheese.

Place the top half of the bread on the filling to complete the sandwich.

Serve the Grilled Picanha Sandwich immediately, and enjoy the rich flavors of grilled picanha with the zesty chimichurri sauce in a delightful sandwich.

Brazilian Spiced Grilled Cauliflower

Ingredients:

- 1 large head of cauliflower, cut into florets
- 2 tablespoons olive oil
- 2 teaspoons ground cumin
- 2 teaspoons smoked paprika
- 1 teaspoon garlic powder
- 1 teaspoon onion powder
- 1/2 teaspoon chili powder (adjust to taste)
- Salt and black pepper to taste
- Fresh parsley or cilantro, chopped (for garnish)

Instructions:

Preheat the Grill:
- Preheat your grill to medium-high heat.

Prepare the Cauliflower:
- Cut the cauliflower into florets, ensuring they are of similar size for even cooking.

Make the Spice Mix:
- In a small bowl, mix together olive oil, ground cumin, smoked paprika, garlic powder, onion powder, chili powder, salt, and black pepper to create a spice mix.

Coat the Cauliflower:
- Place the cauliflower florets in a large bowl. Drizzle the spice mix over the cauliflower and toss until the florets are evenly coated.

Grill the Cauliflower:
- Place the seasoned cauliflower on the preheated grill. Grill for about 10-15 minutes, turning occasionally, or until the cauliflower is tender and has nice grill marks.

Check for Doneness:
- Pierce the cauliflower with a fork to check for tenderness. It should be cooked but still have a slight crunch.

Remove from Grill:
- Once grilled to perfection, remove the cauliflower from the grill.

Garnish and Serve:

- Transfer the grilled cauliflower to a serving platter. Sprinkle with chopped fresh parsley or cilantro for garnish.

Enjoy:
- Serve the Brazilian Spiced Grilled Cauliflower hot as a flavorful and healthy side dish. The combination of spices adds a unique twist to the cauliflower's natural sweetness, making it a delicious addition to your Brazilian-inspired meal.

Churrasco Beef Kebabs

Ingredients:

For the Marinade:

- 1.5 pounds beef sirloin or flank steak, cut into cubes
- 1/4 cup olive oil
- 2 tablespoons red wine vinegar
- 4 cloves garlic, minced
- 1 tablespoon smoked paprika
- 1 tablespoon ground cumin
- 1 teaspoon dried oregano
- 1 teaspoon onion powder
- 1 teaspoon chili powder
- Salt and black pepper to taste

For the Kebabs:

- Cherry tomatoes
- Red and green bell peppers, cut into chunks
- Red onions, cut into wedges
- Wooden or metal skewers (if using wooden skewers, soak them in water for at least 30 minutes)

Instructions:

Prepare the Marinade:
- In a bowl, whisk together olive oil, red wine vinegar, minced garlic, smoked paprika, ground cumin, dried oregano, onion powder, chili powder, salt, and black pepper.

Marinate the Beef:
- Place the beef cubes in a large bowl or resealable plastic bag. Pour the marinade over the beef and ensure each cube is well-coated. Marinate for at least 1-2 hours in the refrigerator, or preferably overnight for maximum flavor.

Assemble the Kebabs:

- Preheat your grill to medium-high heat.
- Thread the marinated beef cubes, cherry tomatoes, bell pepper chunks, and red onion wedges onto the skewers, alternating between the ingredients.

Grill the Kebabs:
- Place the assembled kebabs on the preheated grill. Grill for about 10-15 minutes, turning occasionally, or until the beef reaches your desired level of doneness and the vegetables are tender and slightly charred.

Check for Doneness:
- Ensure the beef is cooked to your liking. It's recommended to use a meat thermometer to check for doneness (145°F/63°C for medium-rare, 160°F/71°C for medium).

Remove from Grill:
- Once grilled to perfection, remove the Churrasco Beef Kebabs from the grill.

Serve:
- Arrange the kebabs on a serving platter.

Garnish (Optional):
- Garnish with additional fresh herbs or a drizzle of olive oil if desired.

Enjoy:
- Serve the Churrasco Beef Kebabs hot and enjoy the delicious blend of flavors from the marinated beef and grilled vegetables. This dish captures the essence of Brazilian churrasco in a convenient and flavorful kebab form.

Brazilian Guava Glazed Chicken Wings

Ingredients:

For the Chicken Wings:

- 2 pounds chicken wings, split at joints, tips discarded
- Salt and black pepper to taste
- 1 tablespoon olive oil

For the Guava Glaze:

- 1 cup guava paste, melted
- 1/4 cup soy sauce
- 1/4 cup honey
- 2 tablespoons apple cider vinegar
- 2 cloves garlic, minced
- 1 teaspoon ground cumin
- 1 teaspoon smoked paprika
- 1/2 teaspoon cayenne pepper (adjust to taste)
- Sesame seeds and chopped cilantro for garnish (optional)

Instructions:

Preheat the Oven:
- Preheat your oven to 400°F (200°C).

Prepare the Chicken Wings:
- Pat the chicken wings dry with paper towels. Season them with salt and black pepper.

Bake the Chicken Wings:
- Place the seasoned chicken wings on a baking sheet lined with parchment paper. Drizzle with olive oil and toss to coat. Bake in the preheated oven for about 40-45 minutes or until the wings are golden brown and crispy, turning them halfway through the cooking time.

Make the Guava Glaze:
- In a saucepan over medium heat, combine melted guava paste, soy sauce, honey, apple cider vinegar, minced garlic, ground cumin, smoked paprika,

and cayenne pepper. Stir well and let it simmer for 5-7 minutes until the glaze thickens slightly.

Glaze the Chicken Wings:
- Once the chicken wings are cooked, transfer them to a large bowl. Pour the guava glaze over the wings and toss to coat them evenly.

Broil for Caramelization:
- Preheat the broiler. Place the glazed wings back on the baking sheet and broil for 2-3 minutes until the glaze caramelizes slightly. Keep an eye on them to prevent burning.

Check for Doneness:
- Ensure the chicken wings are glazed and have a caramelized finish.

Garnish (Optional):
- Sprinkle sesame seeds and chopped cilantro over the glazed wings for added flavor and presentation.

Serve:
- Arrange the Brazilian Guava Glazed Chicken Wings on a serving platter.

Enjoy:
- Serve the chicken wings hot, and enjoy the sweet and savory flavors of the guava glaze. This dish is a unique and delicious twist on classic chicken wings, inspired by Brazilian flavors.

Grilled Brazilian Sardines

Ingredients:

- 1 pound fresh sardines, cleaned and gutted
- 2 tablespoons olive oil
- 3 cloves garlic, minced
- 1 teaspoon smoked paprika
- 1 teaspoon ground cumin
- 1 teaspoon dried oregano
- 1/2 teaspoon red pepper flakes (adjust to taste)
- Salt and black pepper to taste
- 2 tablespoons fresh parsley, chopped (for garnish)
- Lemon wedges for serving

Instructions:

Preheat the Grill:
- Preheat your grill to medium-high heat.

Prepare the Sardines:
- Clean and gut the fresh sardines. Rinse them under cold water and pat them dry with a paper towel.

Make the Marinade:
- In a small bowl, combine olive oil, minced garlic, smoked paprika, ground cumin, dried oregano, red pepper flakes, salt, and black pepper. Mix well to create the marinade.

Coat the Sardines:
- Place the sardines in a shallow dish. Brush the marinade over the sardines, ensuring they are well-coated on both sides. Allow them to marinate for about 15-20 minutes.

Grill the Sardines:
- Place the marinated sardines on the preheated grill. Grill for about 2-3 minutes per side or until the sardines are cooked through and have nice grill marks.

Check for Doneness:
- Ensure the sardines are cooked, and the flesh flakes easily with a fork.

Remove from Grill:
- Once grilled to perfection, remove the sardines from the grill.

Garnish and Serve:
- Sprinkle chopped fresh parsley over the grilled sardines for garnish.

Serve with Lemon Wedges:
- Serve the Grilled Brazilian Sardines hot with lemon wedges on the side.

Enjoy:
- Enjoy the Grilled Brazilian Sardines as a delicious and flavorful seafood dish. The combination of spices and grilling enhances the natural taste of the sardines, creating a delightful and authentic Brazilian experience.

Brazilian Pork Tenderloin with Mango Salsa

Ingredients:

For the Pork Tenderloin:

- 2 pork tenderloins
- 2 tablespoons olive oil
- 4 cloves garlic, minced
- 1 tablespoon ground cumin
- 1 tablespoon smoked paprika
- 1 teaspoon dried oregano
- Salt and black pepper to taste

For the Mango Salsa:

- 2 ripe mangoes, peeled, pitted, and diced
- 1/2 red onion, finely chopped
- 1 red bell pepper, diced
- 1 jalapeño, seeded and minced
- Juice of 2 limes
- 1/4 cup fresh cilantro, chopped
- Salt and black pepper to taste

Instructions:

Pork Tenderloin:

> Preheat the Oven:
> - Preheat your oven to 400°F (200°C).
>
> Prepare the Pork Tenderloin:
> - Pat the pork tenderloins dry with paper towels. Season them with salt and black pepper.
>
> Make the Spice Rub:
> - In a small bowl, mix together minced garlic, ground cumin, smoked paprika, dried oregano, and olive oil to create a spice rub.
>
> Rub the Spice Mix:

- Rub the spice mix over the pork tenderloins, ensuring they are well-coated.

Sear the Pork:
- Heat an oven-safe skillet over medium-high heat. Sear the pork tenderloins on all sides until browned.

Finish in the Oven:
- Transfer the skillet to the preheated oven and roast for about 15-20 minutes or until the internal temperature reaches 145°F (63°C).

Rest and Slice:
- Allow the pork tenderloins to rest for a few minutes before slicing them into medallions.

Mango Salsa:

Prepare the Mango Salsa:
- In a bowl, combine diced mangoes, finely chopped red onion, diced red bell pepper, minced jalapeño, lime juice, chopped cilantro, salt, and black pepper. Mix well.

Adjust Seasoning:
- Adjust the seasoning of the salsa to taste, adding more salt, pepper, or lime juice if needed.

Serve:

Plate the Pork:
- Arrange the sliced pork tenderloin medallions on a serving platter.

Top with Mango Salsa:
- Spoon the flavorful mango salsa over the pork tenderloin medallions.

Garnish (Optional):
- Garnish with additional cilantro if desired.

Enjoy:
- Serve the Brazilian Pork Tenderloin with Mango Salsa hot and savor the succulent and spiced pork complemented by the vibrant and refreshing mango salsa. This dish offers a burst of Brazilian-inspired flavors.

Churrasco-Style Grilled Potatoes

Ingredients:

- 2 pounds baby potatoes, halved
- 3 tablespoons olive oil
- 4 cloves garlic, minced
- 1 teaspoon dried oregano
- 1 teaspoon smoked paprika
- 1 teaspoon ground cumin
- Salt and black pepper to taste
- Fresh parsley, chopped (for garnish)
- Lemon wedges for serving

Instructions:

Preheat the Grill:
- Preheat your grill to medium-high heat.

Parboil the Potatoes:
- In a pot of salted boiling water, parboil the halved baby potatoes for about 5-7 minutes, just until they are slightly tender but not fully cooked.

Make the Marinade:
- In a small bowl, mix together olive oil, minced garlic, dried oregano, smoked paprika, ground cumin, salt, and black pepper to create the marinade.

Coat the Potatoes:
- Drain the parboiled potatoes and place them in a large bowl. Pour the marinade over the potatoes and toss until each piece is well-coated.

Skewer the Potatoes:
- Thread the marinated potatoes onto skewers, ensuring they are evenly distributed.

Grill the Potatoes:
- Place the skewered potatoes on the preheated grill. Grill for about 10-15 minutes, turning occasionally, or until the potatoes are golden brown and have nice grill marks.

Check for Doneness:
- Pierce the potatoes with a fork to check for tenderness. They should be crispy on the outside and tender on the inside.

Remove from Grill:

- Once grilled to perfection, remove the Churrasco-Style Grilled Potatoes from the skewers.

Garnish with Fresh Parsley:
- Sprinkle chopped fresh parsley over the grilled potatoes for garnish.

Serve with Lemon Wedges:
- Serve the Churrasco-Style Grilled Potatoes hot with lemon wedges on the side.

Enjoy:
- Enjoy these flavorful grilled potatoes as a delicious side dish, bringing the essence of churrasco-style cooking to your table.

Brazilian Cinnamon Sugar Grilled Bananas

Ingredients:

- 4 ripe bananas, peeled and halved lengthwise
- 2 tablespoons unsalted butter, melted
- 2 tablespoons brown sugar
- 1 teaspoon ground cinnamon
- Pinch of salt
- Vanilla ice cream (optional, for serving)

Instructions:

Preheat the Grill:
- Preheat your grill to medium-high heat.

Prepare the Bananas:
- Peel the bananas and cut them in half lengthwise.

Make the Cinnamon Sugar Mix:
- In a small bowl, mix together melted butter, brown sugar, ground cinnamon, and a pinch of salt.

Coat the Bananas:
- Brush the cut sides of the bananas with the cinnamon sugar mixture, ensuring they are well-coated.

Grill the Bananas:
- Place the bananas on the preheated grill, cut side down. Grill for about 2-3 minutes until they have grill marks and are slightly caramelized.

Flip and Grill:
- Flip the bananas and brush the skin side with the cinnamon sugar mixture. Grill for an additional 2-3 minutes until the bananas are tender.

Check for Caramelization:
- Ensure the bananas have a caramelized exterior and are heated through.

Remove from Grill:
- Once grilled to perfection, remove the Brazilian Cinnamon Sugar Grilled Bananas from the grill.

Serve:
- Serve the grilled bananas on a plate, drizzling any remaining cinnamon sugar mixture over the top.

Optional:

- Serve with a scoop of vanilla ice cream for an extra decadent treat.

Enjoy:
- Enjoy these Brazilian-inspired grilled bananas as a delightful dessert or snack, featuring the warm flavors of cinnamon and caramelized sugar.

Churrasco-Style Grilled Mushrooms

Ingredients:

- 1 pound cremini or button mushrooms, cleaned and stems trimmed
- 3 tablespoons olive oil
- 3 cloves garlic, minced
- 1 tablespoon fresh parsley, chopped
- 1 teaspoon dried oregano
- 1 teaspoon smoked paprika
- Salt and black pepper to taste
- Lemon wedges for serving

Instructions:

Preheat the Grill:
- Preheat your grill to medium-high heat.

Prepare the Mushrooms:
- Clean the mushrooms and trim the stems if needed.

Make the Marinade:
- In a bowl, mix together olive oil, minced garlic, chopped fresh parsley, dried oregano, smoked paprika, salt, and black pepper to create the marinade.

Coat the Mushrooms:
- Place the mushrooms in a large bowl. Pour the marinade over the mushrooms and toss until each mushroom is well-coated.

Skewer the Mushrooms:
- Thread the marinated mushrooms onto skewers, ensuring they are evenly distributed.

Grill the Mushrooms:
- Place the skewered mushrooms on the preheated grill. Grill for about 8-10 minutes, turning occasionally, or until the mushrooms are tender and have nice grill marks.

Check for Doneness:
- Pierce the mushrooms with a fork to check for tenderness. They should be cooked through and flavorful.

Remove from Grill:
- Once grilled to perfection, remove the Churrasco-Style Grilled Mushrooms from the skewers.

Serve:

- Serve the grilled mushrooms on a platter.

Garnish (Optional):
- Garnish with additional fresh parsley if desired.

Serve with Lemon Wedges:
- Serve the Churrasco-Style Grilled Mushrooms hot with lemon wedges on the side.

Enjoy:
- Enjoy these flavorful grilled mushrooms as a tasty and savory side dish or appetizer, bringing the essence of churrasco-style cooking to your table.